JOSHUA'S CONQUEST

JOSHUA'S CONQUEST
Was it moral?
What does it say to us today?

PETER MASTERS

THE WAKEMAN TRUST, LONDON

JOSHUA'S CONQUEST
© Peter Masters 2005

THE WAKEMAN TRUST
(Wakeman Trust is a UK Registered Charity)

UK Registered Office
38 Walcot Square
London SE11 4TZ

US Office
300 Artino Drive
Oberlin, OH 44074-1263
Website: www.wakemantrust.org

ISBN 1 870855 46 9

Cover design by Andrew Owen
Cover illustration from Matthaeus Merian the Elder, 'The Fall of Jericho'

Printed by Stephens & George, Merthyr Tydfil, UK

Contents

1   Attitudes for Christian Living   9
    Joshua 1 – 2

2   Blessing Requires Holiness   23
    Joshua 3 – 6

3   The Sin of Achan   41
    Joshua 7

4   The Morality of Israel's Wars   55
    Joshua 8 – 10

5   The Lord's Strategy Proved   71
    Joshua 11

6   Truly Believing   87
    Joshua 17 – 20

7   Loyalty and Accountability   101
    Joshua 22 – 24

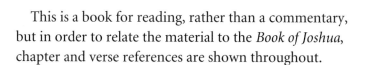

This is a book for reading, rather than a commentary, but in order to relate the material to the *Book of Joshua,* chapter and verse references are shown throughout.

Not all of *Joshua* is covered (such as the allocation of the land) and little attention is given to the geography of the battles, because the aim is to bring out the spiritual message for today, and to explain the 'problem' portions and passages which evoke questions on, for example, the morality of so much killing, and the apparent responsibility of God in hardening the hearts of the Canaanites. (The term 'Canaanites' is used very generally in this book to describe *all* the inhabitants of the promised land.)

Joshua himself is not here extolled as a great general (though he certainly was) because he was guided throughout the Conquest by the 'Captain of the Lord's host', Who both planned and gave the victory as the Israelites obeyed and trusted Him.

Rooted and grounded in love for the Lord, Joshua was utterly faithful, wonderfully stable, and scrupulously obedient. The book of the Bible that bears his name is a magnificent anthology of events to challenge and inspire God's children in every age.

1

Attitudes for Christian Living
Joshua 1 – 2

'Now after the death of Moses the servant of the Lord it came to pass, that the Lord spake unto Joshua the son of Nun, Moses' minister, saying, Moses my servant is dead; now therefore arise, go over this Jordan, thou, and all this people, unto the land which I do give to them, even to the children of Israel' (*Joshua 1.1-2*).

JOSHUA IS VERY obviously a book for the Christian life, full of lessons and parallels for churches and individual believers. It has episodes designed to strengthen those who are young in the faith, and events for the seasoned believer also. This overview will seek to bring out God's purposes in inspiring and preserving this record of events, and to show the kind of application intended for us today.

Chapter four of this book will show the morality of the Conquest, answering the uneasiness and misgivings which believers may feel about these events, and showing the possibilities of divine mercy throughout.

The *Book of Joshua* covers a 30-year period from about 1405 BC. It

Josh 1.1-2 takes its name from the main character, but this does not imply that Joshua was the author. Interestingly, Calvin thought it was written by Eleazar, the high priest and son of Aaron, but we do not really know. The book opens with the commissioning of Joshua, and the renewal and fulfilment of the promise of land to Abraham's descendants. It speaks about the sending of spies, the crossing of Jordan, the Conquest of Canaan, and the allocation of land to the tribes. It concludes with passages of dedication, promise and warning.

We find in *Joshua* the reason why the work of Bible-believing churches today is sometimes unsuccessful, and why individuals often make little progress in their spiritual lives. But *Joshua* goes much further than exposing our weaknesses, for it is crowded with powerful encouragements and promises.

The narrative opens at the very beginning of a new era, as the commission of God comes to Joshua after the death of Moses. Joshua is 84 years old and yet there is no record like his for youthfulness and energy, and this is an encouragement to all of us, telling us that there is no need for believers to lose their capacity and desire to *act* for the Lord, as much as health and ability allow. There is no need to grow cold in hoping and praying either. Here we see an aged man exhibiting immense vigour in the service of God, injecting purpose and passion into an entire nation. We should never allow our fervour in the work of the Lord to diminish.

Joshua No Innovator

In his leadership of the nation Joshua did not start from scratch, because so much had already been accomplished. The people had been brought together, detailed laws had been given, and the manner of worship ordained. Joshua stepped into the shoes of Moses when the most important aspects of national life were already in place, leaving no scope for him to play the innovator's role. He was not the kind of leader who felt he must create something of his very own and so leave his mark on the world. He did not seek a distinctive place in history, and, for this very reason, God gave him one.

Some Christian leaders today do not care for this aspect of Joshua's example, because they want to create new ways, and to become noted for this. Novel forms of evangelism and new ways of worshipping are introduced to the evangelical world at an amazing rate, dramatically overturning the whole established mode of doing things. It is as though some Christian leaders no longer trust the Word and the Spirit, and their pride takes over as they struggle to innovate and leave their mark.

We look around us and see innovations taking place in the churches that would never have been thought of forty years ago, when things were more stable. Yet we are supposed to maintain a biblical tradition, not change things without reason. While Joshua had fresh conquests, he did not invent new rules for the church of those days, and this is the strength of his example. He understudied Moses very carefully, and we should understudy the Saviour and also the pattern provided for us in the methods of the apostle Paul. We should study the *Book of Acts* to see how things were done, and the reasons why they were done that way. We should humble ourselves to appreciate and value that inspired pattern for church life and service.

Early Miracles and their Purpose

'Go over this Jordan' is a tremendous command from God for the opening of Joshua's leadership. Nearly forty years previously they had crossed the Red Sea, that great miracle to crown another – their deliverance from Egypt. At Jordan there was to be a slightly scaled-down reproduction of the Red Sea miracle, to remind the people of their redemption and to encourage them for the great campaign ahead.

Today we look back on a vastly greater miracle of redemption, when the Son of God came into this world, assumed human flesh,

Josh 1.2-4   and went to the cross of Calvary. There He took the eternal weight of punishment for all His people, bearing away its every pang. There He tasted every moment of separation from the Father that His people should have suffered in everlasting banishment, and so He bore away their sin. There He offered up His own life of perfect righteousness to earn the blessings of Heaven for all the redeemed.

If the memory of Israel's redemption from Egypt was so important that they were given two miracles of divided water to keep it before them, how much more important it is for us to remember our redemption accomplished at Calvary. It is by reflecting on this and thanking Him every day, that we are held in our faith and given the strength and assurance we need for every situation.

Soon Jericho will fall, and it would seem so easy. Once ushered across Jordan in effortless safety, only a token act would be required of the people for the defeat of that great, fortified city. The people may then have begun to think that this was how it would always be, and that the coming Conquest of the land would require no effort from them, but God's purpose in the miracles at Jordan and Jericho was to encourage them to trust Him.

All believers share this very experience at conversion, when sin falls very easily. A lady just recently told me of how, when her husband was converted, he gave up his lifelong heavy smoking habit in a day. A man recalled that he was converted as a hopeless alcoholic, and yet his craving vanished in a few hours. This is not necessarily the experience of every converted alcoholic, but in different ways established sins are frequently overcome relatively painlessly at conversion, as the Lord seems to take over the battle against sinful things, and virtually carries us out of the world. However, this does not mean that it will always be easy, because all too soon our very own struggle against sin begins, yet we have the help of the Holy Spirit. In the early days of spiritual life, however, Christ bears the tender lambs in His arms, and so we cross Jordan safely and the walls of Jericho fall before us to convince us of His power to help in the lifelong, future struggle.

It is very often the same with the new Christian's early experience of witness. It seems easy at first to catch a person's attention and to gain a good hearing, but it becomes more difficult as time goes on. The Lord makes it easy at first, just as He virtually carried the Israelites through Jordan and Jericho, and we taste His special power and presence, but His purpose is to strengthen our faith for harder future battles.

The Great Promise of Land

'From the wilderness and this Lebanon even unto the great river, the river Euphrates, all the land of the Hittites, and unto the great sea toward the going down of the sun, shall be your coast' (Joshua 1.4).

The ancient promise of land is now to be fulfilled to a considerable extent. In one sense (Joshua 21.43 tells us), they took all the land; in another sense, much land remained untaken and uncleared of Canaanites (eg: Joshua 13.1). The explanation is that major fortified cities fell, giving control to the Israelites, but numerous smaller towns and areas, and remoter parts, were not taken in Joshua's time. The whole of the promised tract of land did not become a reality until the time of David, and here, surely, is one of the wonders of Bible typology. It was only when David came, a most notable type (or picture) of Christ the Saviour, that the *physical* land promise was most fully achieved, and this was because the physical land was itself a type and token of a far greater and better country, the 'heavenly' country of Hebrews 11.16.

Although the failure to take the land in Joshua's time was due to the failure of the people, God did not overrule their inadequacy, because the physical land promise would not be wholly fulfilled until David, the typical mediator, came.

The land promise to the Jews of old has now been long fulfilled, and also forfeited with the ending of the era of Jewish privilege. The

(Josh 1.4-5) ultimate, complete fulfilment of the promise is
intended for all Abraham's *spiritual* children and will
be realised in the rejuvenated and reconstituted world of purity and
perfection, made for the eternal possession of the redeemed. When
Christ comes, it will be as though Heaven comes down to earth and
earth is elevated to Heaven, forming a physical yet spiritually-
endowed land of unimaginable glory and beauty, radiant with the
presence of Christ for all eternity. Only then will the promise to
Abraham be perfectly consummated.

Returning to *Joshua*, why did the people fail to occupy the land?
One reason given in Scripture is their idolatry. Although they were
commanded to get rid of all pagan idols, they clearly did not do so,
and this obviously frustrated the full realisation of the land promise.
Idolatry is still with us today, as Bible-believing Christians, presenting itself in all forms of worldliness, and leading to the forfeiture of
so much blessing.

But there are other reasons why the Israelites failed to take all the
land, and these are also represented in our individual and church
lives. We may forfeit God's promises of advance because we become
wholly satisfied, as they did, with what we have already. It is as if we
say to ourselves, 'I have been a Christian for many years, and I am
very satisfied with my mediocre level of learning and holiness and
service. Why should I hunger and thirst after more knowledge of the
Bible when I am happy with what I have? Why should I long for
greater instrumentality when I have a manageable measure? And
why should I pant after a more elevated Christian walk, when I have
my lovely home and family, and many treasured possessions to
satisfy me?'

With the Israelites there was much indolence and faithlessness,
and so there is with us. How much we need to pray that we may
press on in personal growth, in the study of God's Word, in zeal for
sanctification, and in commitment to soul winning, examining our
hearts every day, battling against our spiritual lethargy, and desiring

greater Christian character! Let us never grow cold, but long for progress every day of our lives.

Faith Must Have a Focus

God's promise to Joshua is magnificent: 'There shall not any man be able to stand before thee all the days of thy life: as I was with Moses, so I will be with thee: I will not fail thee, nor forsake thee' *(Joshua 1.5).*

Joshua could have so easily been overwhelmed by the vast enterprise before him, and by the many violent tribes in the land, but God said that no pagan king would be able to stand before him. This was a promise that he would rest on constantly, that would always ring in his ears.

We tend to forget that faith must rest on something. Believers should not merely say to themselves, 'I must exercise faith,' because faith must be in or on something. It cannot exist in a vacuum. What is this thing called faith? It is to be *certain* and to be *fully convinced* or persuaded about something. There is no such thing as faith which is not fixed on something. When Joshua needed to be strengthened he put faith in God's clear promise: 'As I was with Moses, so I will be with thee: I will not fail thee, nor forsake thee.'

It must be stressed that the exercise of faith is not a nebulous matter in which we think of a hazy, vague, formless, indistinct hope, but it is an act of fixing the mind on some clear promise or work of God. Joshua fixed his eye on that great promise through every trial and accomplishment of his journey, and we must do the same, consciously trusting the One Who purchased us at such great expense, and His promise to see us through to the end. If we lose touch with His work and promises it will not be His fault but our own. The rule must always be – not nebulous faith, but specific faith.

When faith fails it is because it is not being applied to something definite. If we find ourselves wandering about in the Christian life, it is not that we do not have faith; it is because it is flapping in the

Josh 1.5-9 breeze, attached to nothing in particular. It must be fastened on some promise, some truth, some great theme concerning the Lord, because that alone is the life of faith.

Just as no pagan king would stand before Joshua when faith was exercised, no ideology in the world, no wall of atheism, no level of hostility will prevent us, by the power of God, rescuing souls out of their lost condition, so long as we exercise our faith. The promise – 'I will not fail thee, nor forsake thee,' is united with a response (taken from the *Psalms*) in *Hebrews 13.6*: 'So that we may boldly say, The Lord is my helper, and I will not fear what man shall do unto me.' It is amazing to reflect on this: that the infinite, omnipotent God personally has His eye upon us. The promise is so strong that God's integrity is at stake here. He cannot fail us when He has spoken so powerfully. In the original version of that superb hymn, 'My hope is built on nothing less, than Jesus' blood and righteousness,' there is a grand couplet that you do not find in modern hymnbooks, taking up the matter of God's integrity. If He has made a promise it is inconceivable that He will not keep it, and so the hymnwriter says,

> His honour and His name's at stake,
> To save me from the burning lake.

Duties and Distractions

When the Lord says (verse 6) – 'Be strong and of a good courage,' there is more to this than meets the eye, because 'strong' carries the idea of seizing hold of something. Tenacity is in mind here. The sense is – Be very loyal, unswerving, and thus, 'of a good courage'. The Hebrew translated 'courage' comes from the word to be alert, and this helps us see what kind of courage is in mind. The idea is – 'Don't hide your head in the sand, Joshua, but face up to things. Don't be afraid of your circumstances, but be alert and notice what needs doing. Don't pretend it isn't happening, or that it isn't there.' This is a courage which sees, faces and deals with matters.

Next come yet more terms and conditions attached to the great promise referred to earlier – 'that thou mayest observe to do according to all the law, which Moses my servant commanded thee.' The law here extends beyond the moral and ceremonial law to include the instructions for conquest. Believers must, of course, scrupulously observe the moral law, and all the biblical instructions for the Christian life. Do we wish to be blessed as Sunday School teachers, or as witnesses in our place of study or business? Then we must strive to keep the moral law of God, and also the detailed duties for Christian life and worship unfolded to us in the Scriptures. These include, for example, the rules for reverent, earnest worship. There is a tendency these days not to worry too much about loyalty to the details of God's Word, but without loyalty we lose the blessing.

The solemn words of verse 7 are extremely important: 'Turn not from it *[the law]* to the right hand or to the left, that thou mayest prosper withersoever thou goest.' The implication is that people will constantly want the standards to be relaxed. They will say, 'Let's take it more slowly, let's take it easily, let's avoid the hard thing.' Some will devise alternative ways of doing everything, wanting to imitate the nations around them, but obedience is paramount, and Joshua had to hold the line.

A curious statement occurs in verse 8, when God commands Joshua – 'This book of the law shall not depart out of thy mouth.' We might have expected the Lord to say that the book of the law should not depart from his *heart,* but no, it is his mouth, because Joshua will be teaching these things by his personal example as a prominent leader. He will also be giving instructions that would need to be in accordance with the Word of God. Although not a regular teacher, he will inevitably communicate God's ways in all he does and he must remember that. By this he is assured, 'thou shalt make thy way prosperous,' and so will we, if our lives *teach.*

When the Lord made these great promises, He underscored them (verse 9) with the words, 'Have not I commanded thee?' The

(Josh 1.9-2.1) emphasis was on the 'I'. The Lord says, in effect, 'Consider Who it is Who is making these promises.' Here, then, is a precious addition to what we have said about the exercise of faith. When we fix our faith on a promise, we should consider also Who is making this promise, because a promise is no more valuable than the person who gives it. Among men and women, the one who promises may be unreliable and lack the resources to back his words, and so we do not take him seriously. But with God we may reflect not only on His integrity but also His power and His irresistible desire to perform His promises.

It is Christ, we may say, the great victor of Calvary, the sustainer and helper of mighty instruments in Bible times and throughout church history Who makes promises to His people. It is none other than the kindest Person imaginable Who will never leave us nor forsake us. If we couple this reflection with the promises of God, the soul will soar above every obstacle, and assurance will flourish even in a wilderness.

Zeal of the Eastern Settlers

'And to the Reubenites, and to the Gadites, and to half the tribe of Manasseh, spake Joshua saying, Remember the word which Moses the servant of the Lord commanded you, saying . . . ye shall pass before your brethren armed, all the mighty men of valour, and help them' *(Joshua 1.12-14).*

Before the death of Moses, the Reubenites, Gadites and half the tribe of Manasseh had decided to settle on the eastern side of the Jordan. However, they had promised Moses that they would go over Jordan, fight alongside the rest of the Israelites, and return later. When Joshua reminded them of this they made a grand response, acknowledging their duty in detail and with great vigour and willingness. They already possessed the land they wanted, but they remembered their undertaking and were ready to go.

There is an obvious application to us, because we may have been converted some years, and have received countless blessings from the Lord. We may have found an excellent husband or wife, and have settled down with a family and a home, becoming well established and extremely happy. Now we are in the position of those tribes who had chosen to stay on the eastern side of the Jordan. Like them, we must still go with the rest of the church, visiting homes, seeking souls, encouraging the lost, and doing all that may be required of us in the mission of Christ.

The eastern settlers did not recoil and excuse themselves, pleading that they were building their homesteads, breeding cattle and sheep, clearing and cultivating land, and enjoying family life. They left everything and went instantly, and that should be the Christian attitude. Although we may have been saved for years, we must never allow ourselves to see God's work as an unwelcome inconvenience.

If all believers would only recapture their early vigour and willingness churches would certainly move forward. Does it not shock us to read (in verse 18) how the easterners cried:– 'Whosoever he be that doth rebel against thy commandment, and will not hearken unto thy words in all that thou commandest him, he shall be put to death: only be strong and of a good courage.' We do not for a moment suggest that these words apply literally to the present day, but we see how abhorrent it was to these people to neglect the obligation of God's service, even when settled and comfortable.

Rahab and the Spies

'And Joshua the son of Nun sent out of Shittim two men to spy secretly, saying, Go view the land, even Jericho. And they went, and came into an harlot's house, named Rahab, and lodged there' *(Joshua 2.1)*.

(Josh 2)

The sending of the spies, described in *Joshua 2*, actually took place before the three-day notice of the crossing of Jordan (in *Joshua 1.10-11*). *Joshua 1* provides an overview of the whole situation, then *Joshua 2* backtracks to provide a window of detail. We know this because the spies would not have had time to complete their mission in the three days before the crossing of the Jordan.

Let us consider the sending of the spies. Joshua himself had been

(Josh 2) one of the dozen who went on the mission to spy out the promised land 40 years earlier. Some commentators launch critically into Joshua for lack of faith, saying that the sending of spies arose from his insecurity and fear of defeat. It is much more likely that God told him to send the spies, and for three reasons (at least). Rahab would then be discovered and appreciated, so that arrangements could be made to save her, in accordance with God's purpose.

Also, God knew that the spies would face tremendous danger, find themselves on the verge of capture, and experience remarkable deliverance. Their story would then be yet another encouragement to the people, because they would not forget how God delivered men who were in the jaws of the lion, about to be seized and executed. Perhaps the chief purpose of the sending of the spies was that the Israelites would learn that the people of Jericho were terrified of them, and destitute of morale.

The spies went to 'an harlot's house, named Rahab, and lodged there', and this leads to the debate about whether Rahab was a prostitute or an innkeeper. I have vacillated, finding the innkeeper viewpoint attractive, but right now I think she was a prostitute according to the plain sense of the narrative. What a trophy of God's grace she turned out to be, a Canaanite idolater and prostitute who believed God, and was saved. The spies probably entered her house because it was in the wall of the city and afforded a possible way of escape, but it was obviously God Who guided them.

The faith and actions of Rahab are well known, but everyone wants to know about her lie. Some excuse her, pointing to her newness as a believer, while others pronounce her not guilty because it was a situation of war and certain execution, and the king's men had forfeited any right to the truth. The most common view is to acknowledge that she lied, and to point out that other scriptures commend her faith, but without including approval of her words (*Hebrews 11.31* and *James 2.25*).

How interesting it is that the people of Jericho knew so much about the children of Israel! The spies learned from Rahab that their nation was famous, and that everyone knew about their history of deliverance from Egypt and experience of great miracles. They also learned that the Jerichoites had been deeply affected by their history, and though it was unwelcome and frightening knowledge, they believed it. This is most intriguing. It certainly shows how wilfully they rejected the Lord and His Truth, except for Rahab who believed, repudiating her past life and sinful culture to put her faith in the God of Israel, and to take the side of God's people. But for us today there is a tremendous impetus to witnessing found in the reaction of the people of Jericho.

We may feel obscure and disregarded in our college or workplace, feeling that people take no notice, and brush us off. We should never believe that. The whole of Jericho knew about the children of Israel, and all the people in the office know about the believer, taking in more than we realise. We affect them more deeply than we know. They observe our behaviour, constantly evaluating us, perhaps even seeking to discredit us in their own minds, but at the same time recognising that we have a real hold on the living God. By God's power there will be some Rahabs who will be influenced positively by our behaviour and words.

Naturally, the 'witness' of the children of Israel took time to make an impact. Some years ago my wife and I were talking about Sunday School work to a seminary group in the USA, and one of the professors said that something had struck him in our approach, and this was the expectation that children's outreach, while having an immediate result, would also have a more significant long-term fruit. The professor said that Americans tended not to think this way, looking entirely for results in the short and medium-term, and the idea of preparing a generation and a community for the future seemed very novel. But the longevity of stored information is seen in the case of the Canaanites, whose knowledge of Exodus miracles went back

Josh 2 forty years to the Red Sea, but a fuse had been lit in the life of Rahab, igniting her whole soul in the course of time. In our witness even the person who seems least affected and absolutely impenetrable will have taken on board much more than we realise of what we say. Who knows how the Lord will use it?

2

Blessing Requires Holiness
Joshua 3 – 6

'And Joshua rose early in the morning; and they removed from Shittim, and came to Jordan, he and all the children of Israel, and lodged there before they passed over' *(Joshua 3.1)*.

THE BLESSING of salvation is a transforming work of God in the heart which no one could ever earn and deserve, and it must therefore be free. However, *ongoing* blessing in the Christian life is dependent upon our concern for living a holy life, by the help of God. We must desire and strive to please Him, or His power and goodness will be withheld from us, and this principle is taught in the chapters before us as plainly as anywhere else in the Word of God.

Obedience and Self-Watch

After three days of preparation the officers went through the camp instructing the people how they should follow the ark for the crossing of Jordan. The ark represented God's presence with them, and also His law, and they must keep it in view. There is a parallel in this

Josh 3.1-5   for us today both as churches and individual believers, for in all we do we must follow the Lord by the guidance of His Word and never go forward without it. As far as the Israelites were concerned, there must always be a space between them and the ark of about a thousand yards, the reason being apparent to them. They must show great reverence towards the ark, no one being allowed to touch it. In other words, they must stand in awe of God, and so must we. But there is another reason for keeping their distance, because if some people crowded round the ark the remainder of that vast company would not have been able to see it, and it was vital that all should be able to see the focal point of their guidance. So, today, all Christians must be able to see the authority for all that we do in the Word of God. It is not just for ministers or the spiritually educated to see the basis of Christian doctrine and conduct, it is for every member of the church to see it. It is not good enough for a preacher to say, 'This is what you must do,' without showing how he derives his teaching from the Word. Believers must be able to see for themselves that it is the Lord's will, and not merely the preacher's opinion. Just as the multitude of Israelites could see that it was not Joshua or the priests and Levites who were leading them, but the ark (representing the presence of God), so believers should be shown God's will from Scripture.

Take the vexed question of worship in our day. Many churches are being ruled by opinion and 'tastes' in how they choose words and music for praise. We read the books of those who advocate the modern style of praise, and we find ourselves reading only their opinions, the 'ark of God' having disappeared. The Word of God is hardly mentioned. Certain Christian leaders are blurring the biblical distinction between things sacred and things profane, saying that there is no difference, and that how you worship and witness for the Lord is just a matter of taste. But there *is* a distinction, and we must follow the teaching of the Word which defines the attitude and culture which are appropriate for worship, and separates these from things which are distinctively the produce of the world, and conform to the tastes of the world. Scriptural principles tell us that worldly-style entertainment music produced for the anti-moral, anti-God, carnal, sensation-seeking crusade of the prince of this world must never be fused with the worship of God. Just as the ark of old would take that fledgling nation on a divinely charted journey, not associating with the debased pagan culture of the land, so believers of our time must follow the Word, not taking on board this world's tastes and delights. We learn from the crossing of the Jordan that God's authority is paramount, but today it is not always in sight.

After Joshua's officers had toured the camp with instructions, he addressed the assembled princes and heads of families, saying, 'Sanctify yourselves: for to morrow the Lord will do wonders among you.' God would work an astonishing miracle, in fact a cluster of miracles, and in preparation the people had to make themselves clean. We do not give enough thought to this today. What does the church do? Do people go out into the community to visit? Are children's Sunday Schools, teenage Bible Classes, and other outreach meetings held? Does evangelistic preaching take place to gather in the lost? Of themselves these activities are not enough, because to obtain the presence of the Spirit working great miracles of conversion, we must sanctify ourselves, and take this very seriously.

Every Lord's Day and, of course, every day in the privacy of our homes, we must sincerely repent of our sins, and promise the Lord we are going to do better. We must give up wrong thoughts, selfish plans, and hostile thoughts towards people who may have upset us in some way. We must put to death lusts, ingratitude to God (moaning about our difficulties) and all self-pity. 'Away with all these things!' Joshua seems to say, 'and sanctify yourselves.'

God cannot bless if His people are entertaining all these wrong things, and not troubling themselves unduly about progress in righteousness. We must give up boasting, lying, unkindness, laziness

(Josh 3.5-8) and all premeditated wrong conduct. If we would only sanctify ourselves and stand apart from worldly talk and tendencies, then surely the blessing would flow among us. Do we prepare for worship, praying for communion and light for ourselves, and salvation for others? Listen to the way matters are linked in Joshua's words: 'Sanctify yourselves: for to morrow the Lord will do wonders among you.' Blessing demands preparation.

The Purpose of Miracles

'And the Lord said unto Joshua, This day will I begin to magnify thee in the sight of all Israel, that they may know that, as I was with Moses, so I will be with thee. And thou shalt command the priests that bear the ark of the covenant, saying, When ye are come to the brink of the water of Jordan, ye shall stand still in Jordan' *(Joshua 3.7-8)*.

It was the time of the year when the Jordan was swollen. The snows on the mountains of Lebanon had melted, and the river had overflowed its banks, flooding the adjacent fields. It was not a matter of the priests stepping down the bank into the river, but of their advancing across gently declining fields into shallow water and then waiting for the command to go forward. The moment they stood in the shallows at the edge of that flooded river, God wrought the mighty miracle that caused the water upstream to stack up. When their fathers had crossed the Red Sea it was different, the walls of water rising on both sides, but now the flowing river was heaped up on one side only, and their track became dry.

The dividing of the Red Sea had taken place nearly 40 years before, and now a similar miracle was given to confirm God's promise that He would go before them and give them the land. For them, Jordan was the second spectacular miracle of crossing water, but today, as we have already pointed out, we have something far greater, the greatest miracle imaginable, the work of Christ for souls. This surely stands out above everything else that we can think of, that Christ came among us to suffer and die on Calvary, bearing away the eternal punishment of sin in a matter of hours, and receiving in His own body and soul the holy wrath of God, in order to avert it from His people. How could anyone stand that weight of punishment for countless millions? Only Christ could do so, Who is both God and man, infinitely strong, and yet truly human. Only He could carry through such a work as an all-atoning death. This is *our* miracle: the wonder of Christ's redeeming work, and this will be the event we remember throughout our lives, to humble us, stir our indebtedness and love, and to encourage our hearts.

If the Israelites had failed to remember Jordan their faith would have surely failed, and they would have been overpowered and crushed by the difficulties which lay before them when confronted by cruel enemies. Similarly, once we forget Calvary, the trials of life will take over and swamp our minds and hearts. We have tasted salvation and proved the blessings of conversion, but we must never stop reflecting on our triple miracle of Christ's incarnation, atonement and resurrection.

The Israelites never experienced another 'Jordan' after this one. Jordan, like the Red Sea crossing of old, and the provision of water and manna in the wilderness, was for *all* the people, whereas subsequent miracles would involve the military component of the nation, and even these further miracles would soon decline. Our triple miracle of the work of Christ, however, lives on because the efficacy of it supplies pardon every minute of every day, and will be the foundation of our eternal security in glory. For us, in its fruit, it is a never-ending miracle.

'Miracles' of a lesser kind do often occur in the lives of believers, in answer to prayer. They do not occur in a constant flow, as some people say, for if the Lord granted His people a continuous flow of remarkable interventions and provisions in their lives, they would no longer walk by faith but by sense. Remarkable blessings serve to secure glory to God, and to strengthen faith – as the crossing of Jordan did, and as the subsequent fall of Jericho did, but such events every day or every week would completely supplant the need to

Josh 3.11-17

exercise patient, trusting faith. The Lord's method is not to spoil but to strengthen us, and so while answers to prayers will be constant, the greater visitations, and the overwhelming blessings, will be much rarer. There is a whole chapter of theology written in *Joshua 3*, with the Lord saying, 'I am doing this at Jordan so that you will remember that I keep My promises.' It is in order that they should remember, not forget and look for some other supposed source of power and comfort.

Further Spurs to Faith

In the eleventh verse of *Joshua 3* there is an important term that really helps our faith – 'Behold, the ark of the covenant of the Lord of all the earth.' It is referred to as the 'ark of the covenant of *the Lord of all the earth.*' This is repeated a few verses later. What a title! Surely this is designed to strengthen faith. To Whom will I pray today? He is '*the Lord of all the earth*', a title that breathes absolute power, ownership and dignity. This is why we advise believers not to be too chummy or familiar in their prayers to the Lord. For example, it is not the best idea to direct *all* your prayers to the Lord Jesus Christ in His personal name, 'Jesus'. It is certainly sensitive, touching and love-expressing at times, but it should not be the normal way we pray, because it does not evoke from us the awe, reverence and respect required by the phrase – the Lord of all the earth. For most of our praying we should address the Father (which effectively addresses the whole Godhead) and revere Him as *our* Father, and yet *the Lord of all the earth.* Reverent prayer is addressed to a mighty Lord Who is not only 'my Jesus' but the King and Lord of all people throughout time. The convention for Christians, laid down in the New Testament, is to address our prayers to the Father in the name of the Son, and this we should *always* adhere to for *public* prayer, and *mostly* adhere to for private prayer. But, of course, if we address one member of the Godhead, we address the whole Godhead, without doubt.

'The Lord of all the earth' refers primarily to Christ, Who is the Creator and sustainer of the whole world. When the world comes under final judgement and is destroyed, He is the One Who will recreate it as the most amazing and beautiful place. He is the Lord Who superintends all things, and the more we can think of Him in His supreme majesty and power, the more our faith and our prayers will come to life. That grand statement – *the Lord of all the earth passeth over before you into Jordan* – is very stirring and helpful to faith.

We should bear in mind that the formidable fortress city of Jericho was only five to six miles from Jordan's river, a fact that would have greatly increased the insecurity of the children of Israel, yet they did not flinch from crossing over virtually in sight of their enemy. They did not say, 'What will happen to us? They will come out of that city in strength and pick us off as we scramble out of the river bed. What will happen to our wives and children?' They clearly believed the Lord was with them, and there was no breaking of ranks.

Every person crossed, and all was accomplished in a single day. This fact produces some problems, because we know that there were at least two million of them, possibly three or four, and it intrigues many Bible students to investigate how long the column was, and how wide. The smallest estimate of the width of the column is sixty people abreast, and the largest figure is six hundred. It is amazing that at least two million people, possibly as many as four million, could be moved to travel so briskly together, none protesting or lingering, and even this is a model for us. If the Lord's people would move together in their churches, thronging the prayer meeting as one, and serving the Lord in harmony and discipline, who knows what could be accomplished!

In a way the priests had the hardest task, because they had to stand in the very centre of the river bearing the ark until the entire party had crossed. They may have eyed the wall of water on one side of

(Josh 3.17-5.1) them with some apprehension, but by bearing the ark stationary in that place they secured the safe crossing of all. Even in the details of the event God was teaching them responsibility and commitment, for they would need to be the first to exercise their faith, the first to enter, and the last to leave. Not until men had come to collect the memorial stones out of the river bed, and placed stones from Gilgal, would the ark borne by the priests leave the scene.

Theirs was a ministry of patience and example, and so is ours if we serve the Lord in any capacity. The Sunday School teacher and the district visitor, as well as the preacher, must exercise prompt faith, great patience and reliability in all circumstances, standing firmly in the middle of the Jordan while everyone else passes over. Matthew Henry says that the priests took a bold step and a bold stand, and that sums up the entire Christian life. By faith we enter the kingdom, and faith and boldness must flourish every step along the journey. We stand against temptation, doubts, trying situations, opposition and scorn, for this is a life of faith.

To remember great blessings is a sure spur to faith, and so the Lord requires a memorial to the great river crossing. Twelve stones (Josh 4) are to be taken from Jordan's bed to be erected as monuments in Gilgal, the next camp before the conquest of Jericho, and twelve from there are to be placed in the centre of Jordan. This is the substance of *Joshua 4* – a grand chapter about memorials. The astonishing day when hundreds of thousands of entire families were taken safely through the river was to be remembered by generations to come, for God is jealous to preserve a record of grace for our strengthening and His glory. *Joshua 4.6-7* and *21-24* should be read by all believers with their own children, and the ministry of Sunday Schools in mind, *our* Jordan being Calvary and conversion through Christ.

In our day we also must frequently sweep aside the clutter of life, pause and remember God's great visitations – the wonderful things

He has done for us as individuals and as churches. We should diary them in mind or book, never taking them for granted. We should give testimony of them whenever it is appropriate, both to the unconverted and to fellow believers, especially our own family, so that those around us may know that the Lord has dealt with us and blessed us.

The Metropolitan Tabernacle portico is one of the great monuments in the Christian church. As we pass by, do we think, 'Oh, I have seen that a thousand times,' looking with unseeing eyes? Sometimes we should pause and think of those days following 1859, when the city was shaken with revival, and countless people saw their desperate spiritual need and came to seek the Saviour. The pillars and pediment of this portico date from the beginning of the awakening, being a witness to it, and constituting a memorial to that season of extraordinary blessing.

The portico is also a memorial to the great doctrinal stand taken by Spurgeon and others in the Downgrade Controversy of 1887, when Bible-denying liberalism entered the wider Baptist community, and Truth had to be defended.

However, we all have individual memorials to maintain in our memories and hearts, of conversion and of many significant, melting blessings of God. We forget them to our great loss, and at the same time we deprive the Lord of our praise.

The Threefold Basis of Spiritual Advance

'And it came to pass, when all the kings of the Amorites, which were on the side of Jordan westward, and all the kings of the Canaanites, which were by the sea, heard that the Lord had dried up the waters of Jordan from before the children of Israel, until we were passed over, that their heart melted, neither was there spirit in them any more, because of the children of Israel' (*Joshua 5.1*).   (Josh 5)

Preparations for invasion occupy chapter five, the first verse being pivotal to all that followed. *Joshua 5* may be divided into three parts, each identifying an essential component of advance. The first is the

(Josh 5.1-9) power of God to influence and to humble people. The second is the necessity of separation on the part of the people of God. The third is the need for reverence and obedience in God's people before He will guide and lead them.

The Lord must first overpower the hearts of the Canaanites if the land is to be taken, because this was a deeply evil society, full of unrestrained promiscuity, carrying out the murder of children on a ritual basis. Lies and violence were the principal means of getting things done. Nevertheless, the Canaanites, by and large, realised that they were soon likely to be conquered, and their hearts melted. They felt the most terrible sinking sensation at the thought of the Israelites, and became utterly demoralised, because God was at work preparing the people for defeat.

In their case hearts were only *negatively* melted, but equally the Spirit of God prepares many for the conquest of the Gospel by first taking away self-confidence, and then implanting a deep readiness to hear. We see around us an atheistic people with nothing but scorn for the things of God and for Christ, but God may move hearts as it pleases Him, taking away the self-confidence and worldly optimism of many. Sometimes He gives people just a little sense of eternity, so that questions about life and death arise in their minds, accompanied by fear and spiritual insecurity. Only God can prepare hearts for the Gospel word. By the preaching of the Gospel we take 'territory' and people turn to the Saviour, but it is the power of God that prepares hearts, and we depend upon that.

The second component of spiritual advance (beginning at verse 2) is the need for separation on the part of God's people, and this involved the resumption of circumcision. So important was the meaning of this rite that it would be carried out regardless of the fact that they were about to encounter Jericho, and the men would be in pain and discomfort in any conflict. Nevertheless, acts of worship and commitment always come first, and Joshua obeyed the Lord. A principal meaning of circumcision (given to Abraham) is that God's people must be a people separated to Him, distinctive and special, and nothing like the pagan tribes of the land to which they went. Secondly, the rite of circumcision also taught that through them and their descendants the Messiah would come. Thirdly, circumcision caused them to look back and see the faith of Abraham, which brought him to be a child of God, setting an example of justification by faith. These three issues were all taught by this rite: the duty of separation from false religion and sin; belief in the coming of Messiah from their nation; and the vital truth that acceptance with God is by faith alone.

Are we separate from this world in our leisure tastes, our lifestyle, our worship, and our attitude to possessions? Surely there has never been an age like the present when the Christian church has been more tempted to adopt and absorb this world, in its affluence and pursuit of goods, let alone in its style of worship. When we read the letters to the seven churches in Asia Minor in the *Book of Revelation* we see how believers in Pergamos, Thyatira and Sardis had fallen to compromise, some eating at pagan feasts, probably to keep their jobs. There was immense pressure on the early Christians of that region to maintain their membership of trade guilds that practised idolatrous celebrations. 'Repent,' said the Lord, 'and all the churches shall know that I am he which searcheth the reins and the hearts: and I will give unto every one of you according to your works.' 'Thou hast a few names even in Sardis which have not defiled their garments.'

In our day, Christians in the West are not under physical pressures to conform to worldliness, but, amazingly, they do so voluntarily. No one forces churches to worship with pop bands and orchestras. No one makes us buy the most expensive goods available for our homes, living as comfortably as we can, and boasting in these things. No one compels believers to go to the cinema, or to parties and dances, behaving as if they were worldlings. The tragedy and shame of today is that these are things Christians do voluntarily, and even

Josh 5.13-15
rush to do. But if we long for instrumentality and blessing, we are to be a separate people. Of course, we will not be separate in terms of not relating to other people, for we want to speak and witness to as many as possible, praying that they might be saved.

Christ's Appearance to Joshua

'It came to pass, when Joshua was by Jericho, that he lifted up his eyes and looked, and, behold, there stood a man over against him with his sword drawn in his hand: and Joshua went unto him, and said unto him, Art thou for us, or for our adversaries?' *(Joshua 5.13.)*

This tremendous event brings us to the third component for spiritual advance – the need for reverence and obedience in God's people, before He will guide and lead them. Christ Himself appears to Joshua, announcing Himself by a divine title. We may be sure this was a pre-incarnate appearance of Christ because the *visible* appearance of God in the form of a man is always Christ according to *John 1.18*, which reads: 'No man hath seen God at any time; the only begotten Son, which is in the bosom of the Father, he hath declared him.'

But why was Joshua alone? Possibly he was surveying Jericho himself, but he was doing so very prayerfully, as at the time of Christ's appearance he was meditating. We realise this because it was as he lifted up his eyes from looking down at the ground that he saw a noble-looking man with His drawn sword in His hand.

If this happened to us, what would we do? Joshua was very close to Jericho where one might think he could be picked off by an archer from the city wall, or a group of horsemen could come out of the city and take him. He was certainly very courageous, possessing a boldness given to him by the Lord Who had said to him, 'You will take this city and this land.' In the light of such a promise he evidently felt safe, but to go up to a nobleman whose sword was drawn and say, 'Art thou for us, or for our adversaries?' reflects immense confidence in the Lord. The protective love of God was around him and he was no doubt very conscious of that.

The Lord's reply – 'Nay; but as *captain* of the host of the Lord'* – could just as well be translated 'prince' or even 'king', and Joshua fell on his face to the earth, and worshipped. The nobleman was not merely *for* the Israelites, He was their Commander-in-Chief, and Joshua would be commander on the ground. Christ would direct everything, and this is exactly how we have to think today. Whatever our church does, and whatever happens in the unfolding mission for souls, the Lord must always be Commander-in-Chief. We see books today coming out in a flood saying that to get blessing, to get thousands of people, we should do this and do that, put on this gimmick, employ that strategy, and the vital question is never asked – What does the Commander-in-Chief say? What counts is not what this or that wonder-working, mega-church builder says, but what the Lord says we should do in His Word. Joshua realised that he must get his entire battle strategy from his far, far greater Lord – 'And Joshua fell on his face to the earth, and did worship, and said unto him, What saith my lord unto his servant?'

The terms for Christ's dealing with Joshua are seen in this response, the first being reverence. Do we fall on our face, as it were? The Hebrew word for 'worship' means to prostrate oneself; to fall before the Lord. This is not the exact posture for worship taught in the Bible, but the worship word tells us that at least we must be prostrate in spirit, or have great reverence.

Never attend the type of church where they dance and sway, laugh and shout, and the leaders on the platform exude confidence, being so full of themselves. Worship is falling down humbly before the Lord. Thankfully we can do this with tremendous joy and happiness, but we must reverence Him by respecting Him, and

---

* This refers primarily to the host or army of angels, who would, invisibly, be fighting for the Israelites, and secondarily it refers to Joshua's army.

(Josh 5.15-6.27) submitting to His will. The mega-church builders are not interested in God's will, for they are too pleased with their own. Even Joshua's reverence proved not to be enough, for the Lord said (as He had said to Moses), 'Loose thy shoe from off thy foot; for the place whereon thou standest is holy.'

Let us always seek perspective when we approach the Lord in personal devotions, never rushing into His presence, unless it is an emergency. We remember He is our Father, and Christ is our Saviour. He has taken our sins, and loved us with an everlasting love, and yet we must seek perspective in prayer, thinking of Who He is, and appreciating His majesty, His infinity, His holiness, and His power. Let us take time to reflect, wonder at His great goodness, and pledge our obedience.

Lessons for Today from Jericho's Fall

'Now Jericho was straitly shut up because of the children of Israel: none went out, and none came in' (Joshua 6.1).

All that Jericho had heard about Israel's miracles and preservation had convinced both leaders and ordinary people that these invading (Josh 6) people were invincible. And yet Jericho would not seek peace, but remained utterly defiant, determined that the God of Israel would never be her Lord. Before looking at the significance to us of the fall of Jericho, we must amplify a point already made about Rahab. It is surprising how seriously our witness as Christians is taken. The people we work or study with, and perhaps even members of our own family, are often 'straitly shut up' because of us. They have their guard up to protect themselves from our testimony, and the doors of their minds are firmly closed. Their portcullis is down, their drawbridge up, because they fear that we are going to get at them, and they know the kind of thing we are likely to say. Sometimes the conversation is just beginning to turn spiritual when the bars and bolts rattle into position, and the shutters are pulled down to shut out our influence. That is how it is.

Jericho – pagan, violent Jericho – had every door shut, because of the Hebrews. But the Prince of the Lord's host says to Joshua, 'See, I have given into thine hand Jericho, and the king thereof, and the mighty men of valour.' He speaks as though Jericho's fall was already accomplished, and so it was in a sense, because if God is going to do something, it is as good as done.

The Lord has already determined that many people over the years will be influenced and affected by us, and that our witness of life and lip will reach into their souls. They are on their guard; they do not want to hear; they will avoid us if they can, but even those who will never be saved will take in more than we realise of our message. We are far more influential than we realise.

Why did the Lord give such a curious ritual for the downfall of Jericho? This approach was very obviously designed to teach His people (right down to the present day) a number of principles. Here are sixteen of them:–

(1) The opening victory would be *entirely the Lord's doing*, showing that the promised land was a gift from God and should be received with gratitude and dedication. Our salvation is the same.

(2) *God's power would be wonderfully demonstrated*, inspiring their faith for the future.

(3) Their *present faith would be tested*, as for seven days they would march fruitlessly round the city. But their faith must not waver because 'by faith the walls of Jericho fell down' *(Hebrews 11.30)*. So our faith will be tested before many conquests will be granted.

(4) Their *obedience* would be tested for seven days, for six of which they would walk in total silence, holding unquestioningly to the strange method the Lord had laid down. So is our obedience tested in the conquest of souls. Will we abandon God's ways for innovations of our own?

(5) *God's handiwork would be magnified* by the seven days of

waiting, during which they would see the entire circumference of heavily fortified high walls, so that on the seventh the action of God would be all the more spectacular. Hard and long delayed conversions, once they occur, show the glorious nature of God's saving work.

(6) For seven days they *must be trained to endure derision* from the walls of Jericho, and this they must do with their minds fixed upon God's word, that He had already brought down the city. We too must be trained to endure scorn and derision.

(7) *Jericho had opportunity to repent* for seven days. Every day the reminder of judgement encircled the walls, but every day any possibility of mercy was rejected.

(8) The oft-repeated complete circling of the wall signalled to both Israelites and Jerichoites *the completeness of the coming destruction.* God's judgement must be proclaimed today also.

(9) The presence of the ark on every circling impressed upon the Israelites *the necessity of the presence of God* for every conflict.

(10) The use of rams' horns with their flat, unmusical sound, rather than trumpets of silver, made clear that *human skill would make no contribution* to God's victory. So today, worship and witness is a matter of sincere hearts and faithfulness to God's instructions, not human instrumentality and art.

(11) The repeated sevens – of priests, rams' horn trumpets, days, and circuits on the seventh day – speak of completeness, for seven is the biblical number of perfection. The repeated message is that God's time for them to repent will have run its course on the seventh day. So we preach that each life (and the world) also has *a set time before accounts must be rendered to God.*

(12) The great shout marked both the *certainty and thanksgiving* of the Israelites. So we, at every spiritual victory, must give God all the praise, taking none whatsoever for ourselves.

(13) The walls fell flat, so there was no mistaking the *all-encompassing, total nature of God's delivering work*, signifying that in the

future Conquest the Israelites should never be content with partial victory or the survival of Canaanites in their midst. So today we do not seek mere assent to the Gospel, but total Holy Spirit conversions.

(14) Jericho was to be burned as *a lasting memorial to the offensiveness of sin* in a debased culture, and today we must keep before God's people the sinfulness and odiousness to God of the old life from which they have been wonderfully delivered.

(15) The spectacular nature of Jericho's destruction would be *a powerful signal to other Canaanites to repent.* They would not be able to blame and hate the Israelites for Jericho's fall, because they did nothing but walk round it. Even to the Canaanites it was an evident judgement of God. Today every true conversion is a divine work witnessing to the convert's unsaved acquaintances.

(16) The participation of the Israelites in marching round the city taught them that there is *something for God's people to do* in every conflict, even though God is at work. Today the principle that God uses human instruments needs to be re-emphasised, as in many churches there seem to be few workers for the Lord. The Israelites walked around a huge city for days, whereas today few Christians will engage in visitation or literature distribution. The indolence of so many well-taught and privileged believers today is probably unique in the history of the church.

Other legitimate applications may also be drawn from the details of the Lord's commands for the taking of Jericho, for this is an event with a meaning and purpose for all time.

3

The Sin of Achan

Joshua 7

'But the children of Israel committed a trespass in the accursed thing: for Achan . . . took of the accursed thing: and the anger of the Lord was kindled against the children of Israel' *(Joshua 7.1)*.

AFTER FORTY YEARS in the wilderness the people of God entered the promised land by crossing the Jordan, and soon afterwards Jericho fell by the power of God. Not one Israelite life had been lost, and surely the people were walking on air at the prospect of a miraculous take-over of the land. But then came a rude awakening: a jolting reminder that their ultimate calling was to a life of obedience and holiness. The sin of Achan brought down the anger of God, to the humiliation of Israel, when a detachment of 3,000 men sent to subdue the city of Ai failed and fled before the enemy.

God is Never at Fault

Joshua rent his clothes in shame and distress, and fell prostrate in abasement and prayer. It was the most terrible shock. The Israelites

Josh 7.1-10   had all the promises of God with them and had wit-
nessed amazing events, but now their whole future
was in ruins, for if they could not quell a tiny city, how could they
overpower ferocious tribes? Joshua's prayer rather surprises us,
because he was such a faithful man, but here he certainly drifts off
course, saying – 'Alas, O Lord God, wherefore hast thou at all
brought this people over Jordan, to deliver us into the hand of the
Amorites, to destroy us? would to God we had been content, and
dwelt on the other side Jordan! O Lord, what shall I say, when Israel
turneth their backs before their enemies!'

He further complained that his nation would be exterminated,
and God would be at a loss to preserve His own reputation. Joshua
was so overwhelmed by the shame of it that he lost his usual godly
logic, concluding that the promises could no longer be kept.

The response of the Lord was very stern (verse 10), implying – 'Is
it not obvious to you that Israel has sinned?' Joshua should never
have thought that the promise of God would fail, but should have
realised that God had withdrawn from Israel because someone had
broken the covenant by treachery.

We are not worthy to criticise Joshua, a great giant of faith, tower-
ing above us in every respect, but he was undoubtedly reproved by
God for suspecting that He could be unfaithful, and this serves as a
warning to us. When things go wrong it is never the Lord's fault. It
is never due to the fact that God has lost sight of us, or that He is
disinclined to keep His promises. The fault is always on our side and
God permits setbacks in order that He may bring about greater faith
in us.

We say this constantly to people who are seeking after the Lord.
There are always earnest seekers for salvation who wonder why they
cannot find, and they become disheartened, thinking, 'I have
repented and trusted in Calvary and yet nothing has happened to
me. I do not sense any great change or any clear evidence of being
saved.' But, we explain to them, the delay is always on the sinner's

side. Perhaps their repentance is not wholly sincere or is incomplete. Perhaps the repentant seeker never confesses the particulars of what he has done and of how he has behaved. Perhaps he has too little shame and so his repentance is only a token act.

Perhaps the seeker has not placed his trust *entirely* in Christ, imagining that his own good personality or deeds will contribute something to his salvation, while Calvary and grace are useful to make up the shortfall. He may think he is better than others and so God will be quite pleased with him. Such confused ideas delay salvation, keeping seekers waiting at the door. They must, of course, depend entirely and solely on our Lord and Saviour Jesus Christ, on His amazing love, on the price that He paid, and on the righteousness He offered on behalf of sinners.

Perhaps the waiting seeker's problem is quite different. His trouble may be that his life is not truly yielded. He feels ashamed of his sin and sincerely repents, but simply has not handed over his whole life to the Lord. There are certain things he is determined to hold on to; certain selfish or worldly ambitions, or unwholesome recreations. He has not come to the point where he will give up everything into the hands of God, so that He can do whatever He wills with him. There are certain things he is determined to hold on to, and he prays, saying, 'Lord, forgive me; I will be Thine,' but the Lord reads the thoughts of his heart which says, '. . . but not wholly Thine.'

Perhaps the waiting seeker does not deeply believe Christ's promise that, if these matters are in place, He will unquestionably receive him; not *may* receive him, but *will* receive him. The delay may be failure to believe the warrant of faith. Whatever it is, the delay is always on our side, not on God's.

'Devoting Away' Things for God

Returning to Joshua, he was peremptorily commanded to get up from the posture of prayer and to deal with the problem, otherwise God would no more be with them. The Lord had made it clear

Josh 7.11-21 *(Joshua 6.17-19)* that the precious vessels of the city of Jericho were to pass into the treasury of the Lord, but everything else was to be destroyed. This would not be true of other places they conquered, where they would be allowed the spoils, but at the very first place, the spoils were to be devoted to the Lord.

The 'accursed thing' in the *KJV* is translated 'devoted thing' by modern versions, and yet this is not quite right, because the Hebrew refers to something which is devoted negatively, or devoted away. When we give our life to the Lord, we continue to possess it, but we live for Him. However, if we 'devote away' something, it means we have nothing further to do with it, for His sake. From Jericho, the things of silver, gold, brass and iron would be given to the Lord, but all other spoil was to be devoted away. They were to say, in effect, 'I devote these things out of my possession, because the Lord wants them out of circulation, out of use and destroyed.'

When we first come to Christ there are certain things we devote away out of our lives, such as selfishness and worldliness. We want all these to go into a no man's land, out of commission, out of use by us. The sanctification of the believer includes the same idea, as certain behaviour is *mortified* or put to death *(Romans 8.13)*.

The special lesson behind the ban on spoil from Jericho was a warning against acquiring the culture of that people. The things of Jericho, the trinkets, the riches, the garments and everything else, represented their godless, polluted culture, which must not come among the Israelites at all. So the people (in the case of this one city) were not to take of these things at all, but Achan had taken them, and this was seen by God as a complete breach of faith. The covenant had been smashed. 'We were in a relationship,' God said, in effect, 'and by this man's act you have broken and polluted that relationship. You have done the very thing I hated; so it is disobedience and it is treachery. You have broken a privilege and a trust that I have given you, for "Israel hath sinned, and they have also transgressed my covenant".' God's charges speak as though there were numerous people involved in the crime even though there was only one, to show that serious individual sin against His cause is the concern of everyone. There must be mutual admonition in congregations, and discipline for every member whose conduct discredits the cause of Christ. God's charge sheet against Achan includes the words – 'And they have put it even among their own stuff.' They have taken the forbidden spoil as their own, polluting their own things with the things of Jericho.

God's description of the sin brings out its full ugliness, and this also provides us today with a way of looking at our personal sinful tendencies. If only we would pause to get a clear view of how our sinful traits betray God's goodness to us, we would be moved to combat them more zealously. We would more frequently recoil from the wrong things we were about to do or say.

What did Achan think he was doing when he looted the spoil? He brought about a terrible setback to the camp, leading to 36 deaths and many other serious problems. He caused God to withdraw from His people so that there could be no blessing and victory until his crime was expunged. He crippled the reputation of the children of Israel, and brought discredit on the honourable name of the Lord Himself. He made the enemy very bold and potentially set an appalling example and snare to others.

What was this accursed thing? Achan's confession (verse 21) tells all: 'When I saw among the spoils a goodly Babylonish garment, and two hundred shekels of silver, and a wedge of gold . . . I coveted them, and took them; and, behold, they are hid in the earth in the midst of my tent.' The garment refers to a rich princely robe, probably woven with an amount of gold thread, and studded with gem stones. This was clearly for show. Achan thought life would change one day soon, and, instead of being very simply robed, there would be liberty to don all kinds of rich costumes and then he would look so good. It would seem that he had a high opinion of himself and

Josh 7.13-24 felt he merited something princely that others would not be able to match. Covetousness is usually an outcrop of pride. Achan was not entirely alone in his sin, because in due course his family was punished with him, which suggests their involvement, if not in the lust, then in covering up the deed and providing evasive lies. Covetousness often infects others, including those nearest and dearest to the offender.

Thinking of today, pride and covetousness is not only the sin of individuals, but appears at church level also. It is easy to speak of others rather than ourselves, but it is astonishing to see what goes on in some of the so-called mega-churches, where the most opulent premises imaginable are constructed, equipped with incredibly luxurious facilities for entertainment and leisure. The degree of finery is only the princely robe of Achan appearing once again. The pastor and the board of elders spread the covetous spirit, and the people put up the money to make a tremendous show with their 'Crystal Cathedrals' and similar showpieces.

We observe also the great stars of the charismatic movement, who boast in their magazines of their outstanding giftedness, build for themselves multi-millionaire homes, and live for self-advertisement. Achan is their unacknowledged patron saint, and one day God will call them to order and expose their insincerity.

We should prefer godly simplicity as our forebears did. Pictures of the Metropolitan Tabernacle in Spurgeon's time show a very large but essentially simple preaching box, with two tiers of oval gallery running all the way round, and with plastered walls and match-boarding beneath a wainscot. It was fashioned to offer no distractions to worshippers, but to magnify the clear sound of the preaching of God's Word. Simplicity was their watchword.

Ultimately, it was the lifestyle of Jericho that Achan wanted, which proved so offensive to God. Once we are converted we must never let the world back in. The things we used to do, long for, and aim at are gone, and we are different people. The Jericho culture is to be devoted away, and never desired, because this would not only be covetousness and pride, deceitfulness and self-justification, but would betray the divine covenant by which we stand, and inflict great injury on the cause of Christ.

Achan's Scope to Repent

Was Achan given time or opportunity to repent before judgement fell? Of course he was, for the record says: 'Up, sanctify the people, and say, Sanctify yourselves against to morrow: for thus saith the Lord God of Israel, There is an accursed thing in the midst of thee, O Israel: thou canst not stand before thine enemies, until ye take away the accursed thing from among you.'

From the moment of that announcement Achan could and should have repented. He should have rushed to produce the offending articles and offer them for destruction. If he had done so, possibly he would have been forgiven and his life saved. We believe this was likely because the warning of God said that punishment would come upon him *if he was taken with these things*, the implication being that if he offered them up freely in good time, there would have been forgiveness for him.

As the wheels of discovery turned through lots cast at tribal, family and sub-family levels, would not Achan have grown increasingly anxious? Surely an inner voice was saying, 'Do not wait Achan, go forward, and give these things up as soon as you can.' But however alarmed he may have been, because of the stubbornness of sin, he would not relent. Once covetousness gets its tentacles round us, we cling on to our possessions and desires even against our own interests.

Achan had probably justified his sin in his own mind, and certainly minimised it. 'It is only a garment,' he doubtless reasoned; 'it is only a certain amount of money. I have been in the wilderness all these years, and had a hard time. I have gone without. Surely this is only small compensation. And it is not for me anyway, as I will need

Josh 7.19-26 to provide for my children in the new land.' If he reasoned along these lines, he beguiled himself until it was too late for his disaster to be averted.

It is a warning to us, because if we play with earthly toys, and drop the standards of Christian living, material things will quickly hold us in a vice-like grip. For Achan, it was too late all too soon and he was identified as the offender. 'And Joshua said unto Achan, My son, give, I pray thee, glory to the Lord God of Israel, and make confession unto him; and tell me now what thou hast done; hide it not from me.'

If it was too late for his life to be saved, why the call for a full and frank confession? Joshua's pastoral heart was at work, because although a late confession would not save Achan's life, it may have secured for him a safe passage into Heaven. It was too late for an honoured life and instrumentality for the Lord on earth, but Heaven's mercy still lay open before him.

In favour of Achan we must say he prayed a model prayer of repentance, confessing the details of his fully-acknowledged crime. He did not die obdurate and embittered, but chastened and sorry. 'I see my sin,' Achan seems to have said. 'I see what I have done. I have sinned against a merciful and wonderful Lord Who brought me on this great journey, on this historic mission into the promised land across the Jordan, and has promised us life and happiness and glory. And I betrayed Him and sinned against Him.' This is how we have to see our sin also. It is against the Lord. How can we do things against a Saviour Who has borne the rigours and torments of hell for us? How can we shame the mission of Christ? As we said before, to see sin in all its despicable character is to want to put it to death.

Is there in Achan's repentance a pattern of procedure for us? Yes there is, especially in his acceptance of responsibility, for he said: 'When I saw among the spoils a goodly Babylonish garment . . . I coveted them.' We too should track the sequence of our sin. I have done this, we may reflect, but why did I do it? 'I did it, Lord, because

I was so proud. I did it, Lord, because I was so greedy. I did it because of my darkened self-seeking heart. Lord, I repent of the state I am in, and of the attitude of heart that led me to the deed.' Achan in his moment of judgement repented better than we often do. We mumble a generality, while he spelled out the detail.

When Joshua despatched messengers to collect Achan's spoil, they ran, but why? Not out of mere curiosity, we believe, but because they realised the sooner the accursed thing could be got out of the camp the sooner the blessing of God would return. And that is a lesson for us also, telling us to repent as soon as we can and get rid of our offences, changing our conduct and disposing of any coveted thing, so that blessing may return to us.

They then took Achan and all that was his, and 'brought them unto the valley of Achor', literally the valley of trouble, but it was not given that name until this event. That name would always remind them of the trouble that they fell into and the tremendous shame that came upon them, because someone took the things that should have been 'devoted away'.

Did Achan have the problem of total unbelief? Probably not. It is more likely that he believed the warning of God, but chose to 'unbelieve' it. This is how it might work in our case. We say to ourselves, 'I believe that God will withdraw His blessing from me if I sin. However, I do not think He will do that over this particular sin.' By this selective thinking we 'unbelieve' the warnings of God. We no longer attach importance to the issue. To commit any sin we must find a way to unbelieve God's warnings. But if ever we find our minds taking this route we must urgently and decisively stop the process and consciously reaffirm our belief that all God's standards and warnings must be believed.

Achan's princely robe cost him his life. He lost a potentially productive life in the Lord's service, he brought great hurt upon Israel, he struck at God's glory, he hurt the reputation of the people greatly, and worst of all he defiled and broke the covenant. He had

(Josh 7.26) to be executed on account of all these crimes, and while it may sound severe to us, God, through his condemnation, was teaching His people in future ages that His divine honour and the reputation and purity of the church must be preserved. It is said that 'All Israel stoned him with stones,' indicating that all the representative heads of families, however regretfully, affirmed the rightness of the discipline.

Priorities in Discipline

These are still the most important factors in church discipline, and we now apply these in a brief digression on exclusion from church membership today. In the rare event of someone having to be put out of a fellowship for some conspicuously serious sin, a meeting of members is usually held to expel that person. But some have the idea that they will be voting to say whether they agree that the offending member should be put out or not. This, however, is not why the church votes. It is not to decide whether or not we think expulsion is a good idea. If it is clear the offence has been committed – say, fornication – the vote is held for all to affirm that they will sever their connection with the offender in obedience to the Lord's instructions in His Word. It is not so much a *decision*, but a *united affirmation* of the membership to obey God. Of course, if it is not clear that the offence has been committed, then members should not support an exclusion, but, if it is clear, the vote becomes an affirmation that all will follow the rule, however sad the situation.

While on this sad topic, we should be clear what the Lord's priorities are in church discipline. Some may say that the main purpose is the restoration of the offender, and although this is a noble aim, it is not the chief priority of Scripture, which teaches a vital order of objectives. The first reason for exclusion from a fellowship, on the rare occasion it has to be carried out, is to protect and preserve the honour of God. It is a great dishonour to God when the neighbourhood knows that someone who does a terrible thing is happily kept in a church. It is a disgrace to the name of God. We are here, in the words of an old Confession of faith, 'to indicate the honour of God', and in order to preserve His honour a grievous offender must be put out of the church.

The next reason in order of importance is that the Spirit of God should come once again upon the work of the church. If there is a serious sin and no church discipline, God's blessing is withdrawn. Therefore, to enable the Gospel to be blessed once again to other lives, the solemn act must be taken.

The third reason for exclusion is the protection of vulnerable church members. If a church member has done some terrible thing and is allowed to happily continue in the church, then other people might be tempted in the same way because an appalling example is being set. Younger Christians, perhaps, may more easily fall prey to the tempter. So we are to preserve the honour of God, restore the efficiency and blessedness of the work of the Gospel, and then protect others. Fourthly, exclusion is designed to jolt the offender out of hypocrisy and hardness of heart into repentance and reform. However, important as this is, it follows the other objectives in order of priority.

This is why a church meeting is never asked, 'What do you think about the idea of exclusion?' The church meeting is called upon to make that vital affirmation of obedience to the Lord, by which all say they will obey the instructions of the inspired apostle and discontinue fellowship. If this is not a united affirmation then the effectiveness of the Lord's measure will be lost.

Coming back to the case of Achan, when this writer was a teenager he heard a minister apply his sermon on Achan in the following way. He said if there was one Achan in a church, the whole church would go unblessed. If there was one secret sin in a church, God's blessing would not follow. Was he right? No, fortunately he was not right. If there is a serious sin *known* to the church he would be right. If some serious moral misdemeanour is known to the church and

Josh 7 - 8.19

the church does nothing about it, then obviously the blessing of the whole church will be forfeited, as we learn from the letters to the churches in *Revelation*. But does not the Achan episode show that the blessing of the Lord will be withdrawn because of an individual's secret sin? This is not the correct lesson to draw from the episode over Achan, because in New Testament examples (such as the case of the Corinthian sinner and the offenders in *Revelation 2-3*) the churches are first warned about their danger. If we know about a serious sin and do nothing, we stand in danger of discipline as a church. If we do not know, the Lord will bring the matter to light, if the church is faithful and precious in His sight.

Why then, did judgement fall on an unknowing people through Achan? Because, by the case of Achan, the Lord intended to impress upon the minds of all His people that He knows in detail what each one is doing. Believers must be constantly vigilant over secret sins, whether moral sins (the most serious and deadly of concealed sins) or others such as jealousy, envy, hostile thoughts, covetous thoughts, greed, pride and dishonesty. Secret sins include prayerlessness, where a Christian has not prayed properly for a time, but does not want anyone to know. How quickly secret sins can build up, and so we must be almost ruthless with ourselves in repenting of them and rooting them out. Achan's history tells us that sin conceived secretly in the heart soon rules our actions, controls our minds (even to self-justification and evasion), plunges us into hypocrisy before our fellow believers, and finally wrecks our lives.

'And the Lord said unto Joshua, Fear not, neither be thou dismayed: take all the people of war with thee, and arise, go up to Ai: see, I have given into thy hand the king of Ai' *(Joshua 8.1)*.

Following the judgement of Achan, Joshua was afraid. Normally bold and full of faith, after the shock of defeat at Ai he was greatly

Josh 8

apprehensive, and we can understand why. Was there possibly another Achan in the camp? Would disaster strike again? Would enemies be much bolder now?

Some years ago a very successful boxer, on retirement, told the press that halfway through his career he failed to train properly for a contest, and paid the price in a surprise defeat by a low-level opponent. Ever since that time, he recalled, all his bouts had been considerably harder, because he was no longer considered unbeatable and regarded with awe. Every subsequent opponent believed he could be the next to overcome him, and offered much sterner resistance. Not so long ago the manager of a Premier League football team, formerly at the top of the league, spoke of his team's poor showing in their most recent matches. He put it down to the fact that early in the season they were beaten by a comparatively lowly side, and this gave such fire and confidence to every subsequent opponent that life became much harder for them. At a military level, Joshua was concerned about this very effect, for no longer would every Canaanite tribe find their heart melting for fear, as the people of Jericho did.

'Do not fear,' said the Lord, 'I have already determined to deliver into your hand the king, people, city and land of Ai.' The method to be employed against Ai was an ambush, and from this point Joshua and the people would do far more of the work. It was as though God was saying, 'I did everything at Jericho to encourage you, but now you will engage in fighting, and I will amplify your efforts, give you power, and destroy the enemy before you.' This is exactly like the difference between conversion and ongoing sanctification in the Christian life. To transform the life at conversion is entirely God's work, but in the subsequent walk of holiness there is much for us to do, by His help.

There is a grand old application of the ambush at Ai which sees Joshua as a type of Christ, and this is how it runs:– God told Joshua to mount an ambush whereby a contingent of troops would lie in secret and wait, while the main force feigned a retreat from the town to draw the fighting men of Ai out into the open. Once they emerged to pursue the retreating Israelites, the hidden ambush would take the city, burn it, and cut off any retreat for the men of Ai.

The old teachers would say that God gave Joshua this ambush strategy to make him a type of Christ, and whether right or not, it is a beautiful point. Christ is depicted by Joshua in this way. He also yielded in order to conquer. Just as Joshua ran before the enemy in order to conquer, so Christ yielded and gave Himself up to Calvary in apparent weakness, in order that He could conquer Satan, taking the punishment of sin for His people, and so purchasing their souls and their redemption. How much we should want to honour Him in the fight against sin and the avoidance of everything that He hates.

4

The Morality of Israel's Wars
Joshua 8 – 10

'And it came to pass, when all the kings which were on this side Jordan, in the hills, and in the valleys, and in all the coasts of the great sea over against Lebanon . . . heard thereof; that they gathered themselves together, to fight with Joshua and with Israel, with one accord' *(Joshua 9.1-2)*.

THE CONQUEST OF CANAAN under Joshua's generalship gives rise to doubts and questions in the minds of many people, and we must therefore consider whether it was moral and justified. Critics of religion fiercely denounce the Conquest, regarding it as a wholly aggressive and intensely cruel crusade of genocide. It is claimed that no mercy was shown as the Israelites seized an entire region to which they had no rightful claim. Why, they ask, did all the occupants of city-states need to be slain, including the women and children? A true picture of the reasonableness and morality of the Conquest, including the constant and repeated offers of mercy and peace, can only be gained by examination of a number of Scripture passages. These establish the following facts.

(1) God's decree that the Israelites would be established in Canaan was promised and prophesied from the days of Abraham, and in due time He commanded them to proceed into that land, confirming His will unmistakeably by many miraculous events.

(2) The Conquest was a judgement of God upon an intensely evil society. The Israelites would merely be God's instruments of justice. God would confirm that He was carrying out His own will (rather than the Israelites being aggressive out of self-interest) by taking the first city entirely without their aid, and by miraculously intervening throughout the Conquest (eg: the miracles against the Adonizedek coalition of *Joshua 10*).

(3) The rules of war given by God to the Israelites included offers of peace to every tribe and every city, if they would come under the rule of God, but these offers were universally and vehemently rejected by all, with the exception of the Gibeonites.

(4) The standards that God determined to establish in the land, which were detested and rejected by the Canaanites, were those of the Ten Commandments. These, coupled with the promises and warnings of God, were published by Joshua on stone monuments on Mount Ebal in the centre of the land at the outset of the campaign, showing that the taking of the land was a mission coupled with judgement, rather than merely a land take-over.

(5) In all battles except the first two the Canaanite tribes were the 'aggressors' who struck first, by means of two great coalition offensives, one in the south and the other in the north.

The Historic Divine Promise, Confirmed by Miracles

'And the Lord said unto Abram, after that Lot was separated from him, Lift up now thine eyes, and look from the place where thou art northward, and southward, and eastward, and westward: for all the land which thou seest, to thee will I give it, and to thy seed for ever' *(Genesis 13.14-15)*.

The repeated giving of the land promise to Abraham, Isaac and

Jacob (recorded in *Genesis*) centuries before the Conquest shows that the Israelites understood this as God's decree. The land prophecies are also in *Genesis 15.13-21; 17.7-8; 28.13; 35.12.* In these texts the location and extent of the land is very precisely defined. One of these texts includes the reason why the occupants of the land will be under judgement. God said to Abraham:–

'Know of a surety that thy seed shall be a stranger in a land that is not theirs *[ie: in Egypt]*, and shall serve them; and they shall afflict them four hundred years; and also that nation, whom they shall serve, will I judge: and afterward shall they come out with great substance . . . But in the fourth generation they *[the Israelites]* shall come hither again: FOR THE INIQUITY OF THE AMORITES IS NOT YET FULL' *(Genesis 15.13-16)*. These are important words, showing that God would bring the children of Israel to claim the land when the iniquity of the occupants of the land had reached such a peak that He would allow it to go no further, but would move against them in judgement.

If there had been any doubt in the mind of any Israelite that the nation was being sent on a divinely ordained mission, and not a self-serving 'land grab', the miracle of the Jordan crossing followed by the miracle of the fall of Jericho would have dispelled such qualms. Never could there have been any greater endorsements, for such wonders had never been known by any other nation before or since.

Throughout the remainder of the Conquest, when the Israelites were employed in the fighting, God continued to provide miraculous aid, such as the giant hailstones rained on Adonizedek's coalition, which accomplished more than the swords of Israel, so that God was able to say about all their battles, '*I delivered them into your hand*' *(Joshua 24.11)*.

Amazingly, indeed, without precedent in human conflict, aside from the discipline suffered at Ai, not one Israelite ever died throughout the entire Conquest, for this was God's will and God was at work.

An Act of Divine Judgement

'When the Lord thy God shall cut off the nations from before thee, whither thou goest to possess them, and thou succeedest them, and dwellest in their land; take heed to thyself that thou be not snared by following them, after that they be destroyed from before thee; and that thou inquire not after their gods, saying, How did these nations serve their gods? even so will I do like-wise' (*Deuteronomy 12.29-30*).

These words were spoken to the people by Moses forty years before the invasion to show that this was to be God's judgement on an evil society, and that the Israelites must not be influenced and corrupted by that society. Also, it is clearly stated that God would be the driving force in their Conquest. Moses warned the Israelites that they should never worship God in the manner of the Canaanites – 'for every abomination to the Lord, which he hateth, have they done unto their gods; for even their sons and their daughters they have burnt in the fire to their gods. What thing soever I command you, observe to do it: thou shalt not add thereto, nor diminish from it' (*Deuteronomy 12.31-32*).

In these few verses we see their orders from God set out. The land they were to be given was an outrageously wicked region, where the culture of the peoples was vile in the extreme. We know from various Scripture passages that the degree of sexual perversion was appalling and the violence and cruelty horrific. The gods of these polytheistic people were fashioned by them to their liking, 'permitting' every kind of debased indulgence. Through Moses, a leader and prophet authenticated through powerful miracles, God declared His judgement upon the land.

Another important passage is *Deuteronomy 27.1-3* – 'And Moses with the elders of Israel commanded the people, saying, Keep all the commandments which I command you this day. And it shall be on the day when ye shall pass over Jordan unto the land which the Lord thy God giveth thee, that thou shalt set thee up great stones, and plaister them with plaister: and thou shalt write upon them all the words of this law, when thou art passed over, that thou mayest go in unto the land which the Lord thy God giveth thee.'

Joshua carried out this instruction following the victories at Jericho and Ai, at the very beginning of the Conquest, when he took all the people to Mount Ebal, right in the very centre of Canaan, and held a tremendous festival of thanksgiving, coupled with a solemn ceremony of reiteration of the law *(Joshua 8.30-35).* The bold excursion to the highest peak at the heart of the land signalled their firm conviction that they acted in obedience to God, and that His holy law would be their rule in their occupancy of the land. It also informed the Canaanites of the reason why they were to be dispossessed. It was because they so hated this law and sinned so grievously against God.

Peace and Mercy Offered to Every Tribe

'When thou comest nigh unto a city to fight against it, then proclaim peace unto it. And it shall be, if it make thee answer of peace, and open unto thee, then it shall be, that all the people that is found therein shall be tributaries unto thee, and they shall serve thee. And if it will make no peace with thee, but will make war against thee, then thou shalt besiege it . . .' *(Deuteronomy 20.10-12).*

The detailed rules of war to be followed in the Conquest of Canaan were given by God through Moses, and these contain the very specific instruction to offer mercy to the occupants of the land quoted above. Peace must always be proclaimed in some way, and conditions offered.

Further rules order that aggressive males who are determined to fight, and who reject the offer of peace, shall be executed, but the women, little ones, cattle and everything else in the city should be preserved. This last provision applied to the more distant cities, but the cities of the seven principal nations in central Canaan would be totally destroyed with all their occupants. This however would not be so if they accepted the offer of peace. This peace would be on condition that they submitted themselves to the laws of Israel, the

Josh 8.30-35 Ten Commandments of the one true God, and gave up their idolatry.*

This understanding of the passage is confirmed in *Joshua 11.16-20* where the whole country is referred to, yet the text says: 'There was not a city that made peace with the children of Israel, save the Hivites the inhabitants of Gibeon: all other they took in battle.' The clear implication is that peace was offered to all.

Now we come to a passage from *Deuteronomy 7* which gives rise to troubled questions, yet it is easily explained, and is not as alarming as it first appears. These are God's words given through Moses:–

'When the Lord thy God shall bring thee into the land whither thou goest to possess it, and hath cast out many nations before thee, the Hittites, and the Girgashites, and the Amorites, and the Canaanites, and the Perizzites, and the Hivites, and the Jebusites, seven nations greater and mightier than thou; and when the Lord thy God shall deliver them before thee; THOU SHALT SMITE THEM, AND UTTERLY DESTROY THEM; THOU SHALT MAKE NO COVENANT WITH THEM, NOR SHEW MERCY UNTO THEM: neither shalt thou make marriages with them . . .' (Deuteronomy 7.1-3).

Does this passage not contradict the offer of peace of *Deuteronomy 20*? Not at all, because these verses speak about what will happen after the offer of peace has been rejected by these nations. In these circumstances there must be no further negotiations, concessions, treaties or relationships of any kind. The passage applies to militantly unrepentant Canaanite tribes. We must take the two passages, chapter 7 and chapter 20, together to gain a right understanding.

---

* Some interpreters read the passage just quoted in a rather unsatisfactory way, saying that the offer of peace was only for the distant cities. They claim that there was no offer of peace at all for the central Canaanite cities, but this is not what the passage says. We believe the offer of peace was there for both the distant cities and the central ones. If they would not have peace then there was a distinction to be drawn; in the case of the distant cities, the males only would die, but in the case of the inner cities of the tribes that were worst of all, everyone would perish.

Deuteronomy 9.4 says more about the need for the judgement of Canaanites. These words are spoken to Israel:–

'Speak not thou in thine heart, after that the Lord thy God hath cast them out from before thee, saying, For my righteousness the Lord hath brought me in to possess this land: but for the wickedness of these nations the Lord doth drive them out from before thee.'

This is the reason the Israelites were sent to overpower the Canaanites completely. They were not driven out simply to accommodate Israel, but because they were so evil, and deserved judgement. The real guilt of the Canaanite nations may be established from *Romans 1,* where we read that even people from non-Jewish nations possess a powerful instinct or realisation within them that there is one true God. This awareness is suppressed by sinful hearts, but it is there along with a knowledge of right and wrong. We are never to say, 'But these were people who knew no better.' The whole human race, Scripture teaches, knows better, and also knows from the evidence of creation that there is one God. But the supreme God, maker and ruler of all, is unwanted and rejected, therefore when He acts to condemn man, He is entirely just.

Would anyone in Jericho who repented have been saved? One of the great reasons why Rahab was saved was to show that there was no necessity for all the other inhabitants of Jericho to be destroyed if they also had repented. Of course, it was the Spirit Who was at work in her heart, but her deliverance demonstrated that mercy was available.

The Basis of Mercy and Judgement

'Then Joshua built an altar unto the Lord God of Israel in mount Ebal . . . And he wrote there upon the stones a copy of the law of Moses, which he wrote in the presence of the children of Israel . . . And afterward he read all the words of the law, the blessings and cursings, according to all that is written in the book of the law' *(Joshua 8.30, 32, 34).*

The stone monuments erected at Mount Ebal were, in a sense, the Israelites claiming the land, but there was more to it than this, and

(Josh 8.30-35) we need to explain the event a little further.

First, the Ebal festival was held in strict compliance with instructions, even down to the building of an altar of unfashioned, unchiselled stones (as instructed in *Deuteronomy 27.5*), and the inscribing of the Ten Commandments on whitewashed or plastered stones. A vast concourse of people filled the natural valley amphitheatre between Mount Ebal and Mount Gerizim, and there the sacred words of law, blessings and cursings were read. Everything Joshua did followed the divine blueprint faithfully (and this remains the standard for churches to follow today).

Secondly, worship was placed at the forefront of life. The event gave out this message to the Israelites, and to present-day Christians, that the purpose of salvation and spiritual pilgrimage should never fade from view. Every phase of the journey and every victory must be marked by worship.

Thirdly, Mount Ebal published again the terms of the covenant that God made with them, especially the blessings and the curses listed by Moses in *Deuteronomy 27-28*. Here were the standards His people should live by, with their accompanying rewards and punishments.

Fourthly, Ebal proclaimed not only to the Israelites, but also *to the Canaanites*, God's standards and mercy, inscribed in huge characters on those whitewashed stones. Their response to these would determine the destiny of their tribes.

To crystallise the message of Mount Ebal for us today in a devotional way, the following fourfold counsel is plain: (1) Precise obedience to God. (2) The necessity of thanksgiving for all things. (3) The importance of regularly remembering the standards for Christian living. (4) The duty of witness.

From that day there was a standard flying on the 3,000 foot summit of Mount Ebal. It was as though a great pole had been put up, with an outstandingly conspicuous ensign, like others used in ancient battles, except that this standard was actually carved in stone. But as soon as the Canaanites were aware of the Ebal stones, they became incensed and went on the offensive against Israel.

Canaanite cities were very bad, as we have noted. They were guilty of gross sexual perversion and total repudiation of the moral standards of the Commandments, and we cannot help noticing how close to this scenario we are getting in Britain. All moral guidance has been withdrawn from our schools and replaced by the promotion of promiscuity in 'safer sex' literature officially designated to be given to children. Sexual activity in youth, with guidance on the avoidance of conception, is blatantly supported, bringing us well into the culture of the Canaanites of old. In the 1960s, when the present liberal society and alternative morality began to be promoted, few had any idea it would come to the point where the rising generation would be trained in contempt for the standards of the Bible and centuries of moral culture. How long can this go on before we witness severe tokens of judgement? One can only wonder.

God hated the polytheism of the Canaanites, and He hates modern atheism just as much. He judged them for their promiscuity, and in the realm of sexual conduct our society is becoming almost as debased. They also had child sacrifice and other unbelievable cruelties, and we have (despite the letter of the law) abortion on demand, on a massive scale.

Returning to the morality of Jewish wars, we have observed that mercy was available before the fighting, but was rejected in all cases but one. We know that everything that God does is absolutely just and fair, and we remember that the Israelites did not fight these battles by themselves; in fact at Jericho they did virtually nothing at all. God did everything there in order to demonstrate that this was not only His will, but that it would be accomplished by His direct participation and power. In battle after battle, even where the Israelites had to fight, the lion's share of the work was performed by the Lord, and no Israelite died. God enabled them. Therefore, if there is to be

(Josh 9.1-9) any criticism made of what happened in the Conquest, it must be directed against God, because it was all by His decree and power.

The Gibeonites – an Example of Peace

'And it came to pass, when all the kings which were on this side Jordan, in the hills, and in the valleys, and in all the coasts of the great sea over against Lebanon, the Hittite, and the Amorite, the Canaanite, the Perizzite, the Hivite, and the Jebusite, heard thereof; that they gathered themselves together, to fight with Joshua and with Israel, with one accord' *(Joshua 9.1-2).*

The kings of this great confederacy were inflamed most of all by the religious stand of the Israelites, and their carving out the commandments of their God upon that central mountain. The law and its listed curses were so hated that there would be no question of seeking peace. Not all, however, rushed to fight. The exception was the Gibeonites who used fraud to secure their lives. The relevance of this to the morality of the Conquest is that they stand as an example of the availability of peace.

'And when the inhabitants of Gibeon heard what Joshua had done unto Jericho and to Ai, they did work wilily, and went and made as if they had been ambassadors, and took old sacks upon their asses, and wine bottles, old, and rent, and bound up; and old shoes and clouted upon their feet, and old garments upon them . . . And they went to Joshua unto the camp at Gilgal, and said unto him, and to the men of Israel, We be come from a far country: now therefore make ye a league with us' *(Joshua 9.3-6).*

The Gibeonites were not very far away, about twenty miles from Joshua's camp at Gilgal. Gibeon was a huge city, unusually powerfully fortified, and the Gibeonites were famous for their warriors. It is rather puzzling that such people (they actually had four cities) would be the ones to effectively surrender under threat of invasion, realising they could not win against the Israelites. They clearly believed that whatever Moses had said about the taking of the land would come to pass *(Joshua 9.24).*

Although it was by deception that the Gibeonites worked their way into the favour of the Israelites, they still provide an example of available mercy. The Gibeonites stole their peace, but nevertheless they still retained it even after the truth became known, and were subsequently defended by Israel. The facts are superbly narrated. They organised a phoney delegation of ambassadors from a distant nation, scripting their approach meticulously. They simulated worn out clothes, shoes and equipment and presented themselves to Joshua and the princes to ask for a treaty.

'And the men of Israel said unto the Hivites *[the Gibeonites were a branch of the Hivites]*, Peradventure ye dwell among us; and how shall we make a league with you?' The *King James* translators have worded this very carefully. Modern translations proceed along this line: 'Supposing you are near neighbours. How in those circumstances can we make a treaty with you?' The translators have made up their minds that the Israelites were not allowed to enter into any treaty whatsoever with central Canaanites. The *King James* translation, however, expresses the Israelites' response rather like this: 'If so be you are accepted by us, what form of treaty do you expect?' According to this translation the Israelites were not at all suspicious of the Gibeonite performance.

Realising that Joshua was the Israelite ruler, the Gibeonites turned their pleas to him, and he pressed them to say where they were from. He was probably more curious than suspicious, because if he had been suspicious he would surely have noticed their blatant evasion of his question. They just didn't answer him, saying vaguely, 'From a very far country thy servants are come.' They simply repeated themselves, apparently unable to think of a plausible name of a nation far away. But they were astute enough to use language that would commend them to the Israelites, saying, 'From a very far country thy servants are come because of the name of the Lord thy God: for we have heard the fame of him, and all that he did in Egypt.'

They must have rehearsed this, being careful to keep to old information on Israel's victories, because people from afar would not

Josh 9.9-10.12 have been up to date with the latest events. They had obviously warned each other saying, 'Don't talk about Jericho; don't talk about Ai, for that will give the game away.'

Claiming to fear the true God, they produced their mouldy bread to authenticate their story, and this seems to have moved the compassion of the Israelite princes. Therefore, seeking no special guidance from God, Joshua made a treaty, only to discover within three days that he had been duped, and their tribe was only twenty miles away. Nevertheless, he spared their four cities, to the fury of the Israelite rank and file, but held the Gibeonites closely to the terms of their treaty, which said they must be servants to Israel.

This Gibeonite treaty continued to be honoured for 400 years until King Saul violated it, killing large numbers of Gibeonites, resulting in a three-year famine, a judgement from God Who said, 'It is for Saul, and for his bloody house, because he slew the Gibeonites' *(2 Samuel 21.1)*. Saul's house was duly punished by David (one of whose mighty men was a Gibeonite).

At the time of Joshua, the surrender of the Gibeonites enraged the other Canaanite cities in the region.

Canaanite Aggression — The Sun Stands Still

'Now it came to pass, when Adonizedek king of Jerusalem had heard how Joshua had taken Ai, and had utterly destroyed it; as he had done to Jericho and her king, so he had done to Ai and her king; and how the inhabitants of Gibeon had made peace with Israel, and were among them . . .' *(Joshua 10.1)*.

It is important to recognise that all but the first two battles were actually defensive ones. It was only at Jericho and Ai that the children of Israel could strictly be regarded as the aggressors, and this was by the command of God. After these, the Canaanites came out to fight against them. They assembled themselves in vast confederacies, hostile to any offers of mercy, and detesting the standards of God, and they took the military initiative.

Josh 10

These battles were the expression of their rejection of God, while the Lord, for His part, demonstrated to posterity His condemnation and punishment of sin.

A prime example is the emerging Canaanite confederacy of *Joshua 10*. When the organisers heard that the Gibeonites, who would have been an important component in their joint armies, had surrendered to Israel and agreed to be their servants in exchange for their lives, they decided to punish and destroy them. But the confederacy had not expected Joshua to come to the rescue of Gibeon. Why did he do so? If Joshua had been engaged in genocide and territorial greed, would it not have suited him to see the cities of Gibeon destroyed, and to have his own embarrassing lapse of judgement removed? He went, however, to their aid, clearly because God told him to do so, and because he had a treaty of peace with them. Although they had obtained their peace fraudulently, the seeking of peace was always to be honoured. As we have previously pointed out, the defence of Gibeon demonstrated God's willingness to show mercy to Canaanites. If a request for peace secured fraudulently was honoured, how much more would any direct and open plea for peace have been honoured?

The rest of the Canaanite nations, however, would not give up their evil practices and foul culture. They would not repent; they would not accept peace; they would not on any account accept the rules of Israel or her God, or accept coexistence with them on God's terms. Where we are given examples of the exceptions, namely Rahab and the Gibeonites, we see their lives are saved and they obtain protection. This is the moral basis of the Conquest.

Adonizedek, chief king of the Canaanite confederacy, proceeds against Gibeon in chapter 10, and in the course of the ensuing battle between his forces and those of Joshua, the special miracle occurs of the sun standing still. First gigantic hailstones assist the Israelites, killing the majority of Canaanites (10.11), and then the light is arrested.

Josh 10.12-14 'Then spake Joshua to the Lord in the day when the Lord delivered up the Amorites before the children of Israel, and he said in the sight of Israel, Sun, stand thou still upon Gibeon; and thou, Moon, in the valley of Ajalon. And the sun stood still, and the moon stayed, until the people had avenged themselves upon their enemies . . . So the sun stood still in the midst of heaven, and hasted not to go down about a whole day. And there was no day like that before it or after it, that the Lord hearkened unto the voice of a man: for the Lord fought for Israel' *(Joshua 10.12-14).*

Why did the Lord work such an extraordinary miracle? We will not debate whether it was a miracle of rotation of the earth on its axis, as some believe, or whether it was a miracle of refraction, whereby God bent the rays of the light so that they stayed for an extra day – making a remarkable 'local' miracle. The question for us is – Why was it done? Why was it that God said to Joshua, as He plainly did, 'Call upon Me at the top of your voice in a place where people can hear what you are saying. Then pray, calling on the sun to stand still.'

Firstly, the miracle vindicated Joshua. Unrest was in the air, with the congregation murmuring against Joshua and the princes over their acceptance of the Gibeonites, and no doubt people were further disgruntled when called upon to defend them. A remarkable vindication of Joshua was a special and timely kindness from the Lord.

Then there was a message in the fact that when the Israelites battled to drive back the Amorite confederacy, God gave them twice as long to accomplish their task. This encourages us today, because we learn that whenever we are working for the Lord, and it is absolutely necessary, God will provide us with the needed energy. He will not extend the shining of the sun as He did then, but He will do what that represents by supplying strength to do His bidding. Often, in answer to prayer, this special enabling will see us through times of great personal pressure and hardship.

Another purpose behind the miracle was to mark out this battle as a conspicuous event, printing it more boldly on the pages of history, because here the Israelites were given victory despite being numerically overwhelmed many times. The miracle served as a spotlight to remind them and us that God can overthrow the most formidable powers arrayed against His people.

Yet another purpose behind this miracle is that it placed a conspicuous mark or 'flag' on the event of the protection of the Gibeonites. The Canaanites had been incensed at them and had set out to punish them, but they found that a people under the protection of Israel's God could not be brought down. The Canaanites would not forget the day that the people who sued for peace found themselves under the care of God, while Canaanite troops failed to find even the relief that normally came with the fall of darkness. Because the Gibeonites sought peace and mercy, God fought for them. The miracle of the sun declared to all the other tribes of Canaan that their own condemnation and destruction was wholly avoidable if they would only respond to the peace offers of God.

This miracle had still another purpose because it was a crushing message to sun worshippers, which the Canaanites were. They all believed the sun and the moon were gods, along with everything else in the heavens, and to have Joshua, representing *his* God, commanding the sun to act for him was a demonstration to them that their religion was a fraud and powerless. For them, no amount of calling upon the sun would have checked its course across the sky for a moment. Here was a combined rebuke to them, and an authentication of the God of Israel.

But then the old writers like to point out that this miracle also had a typical meaning, because Joshua is to be seen as a type of Christ. Just as Joshua could cause the sun to shine, so when Christ would come, the Sun of righteousness would arise and a flood of redeeming light would cover the world for a Gospel day, and for the conquering of souls. And this, say the old writers, was prefigured in Joshua.

How hard were those Canaanite hearts! They could witness

mighty things in the heavens, and yet were still bent on destroying the Israelites, rejecting all offers of peace, and opposing their laws. How they hated the law of God! Even miracles will not move determined human hearts.

These passages provide precious information and insight to help us resolve our concerns about the justice and morality of the Conquest of Canaan under Joshua.

5

The Lord's Strategy Proved
Joshua 11

'And it came to pass, when Jabin king of Hazor had heard those things *[that
the south had fallen; the Gibeonite war and the confederacy there]*, that he sent
to Jobab king of Madon, and to the king of Shimron, and to the king of
Achshaph, and to the kings that were on the north of the mountains...'
(Joshua 11.1-2).

THE CENTRAL and southern campaign, seen in the previous
chapters of *Joshua*, was swift. It amounted to a stunning,
disabling blow, but not all the smaller cities were taken, and
enclaves of Canaanite occupation survived. So while the first phase
of the Conquest was decisive for control of the land, it was not
entirely thorough, and could not have been because it was necessary
for Joshua to respond quickly to subdue the south, so that when the
north erupted they would only be fighting on one front. Nevertheless, some of their work in the south had to be revisited in the course
of time.

The eleventh chapter records the northern campaign, which was
much slower and fought against tribes greater in numbers and

Josh 11.1-6 sophistication of equipment. When the king of Hazor heard about the fall of the south, he organised a gigantic coalition to defeat the Israelites. But Jabin – not his real name, but a dynastic title – waited too long before acting, and one wonders why. Was it hostility between his city-state and those of the south that delayed the calling of a northern coalition? Or had the southern campaign occurred too quickly for a reaction to be made?

The most likely explanation is that God put Jabin and the northern kings into a stupor of complacency until it was too late for a nationwide coalition to be arranged. Calvin calls this 'a foolish lethargy', brought about by God out of goodness to His people. By it the Lord held back the formation of a larger enemy army, while significant victories were given in the south to build up the faith of the people. They saw God at work and were then ready for further conquests.

We can apply this to ourselves today. The Lord is understanding of our weakness and will not allow us to be tempted or tried above the point we are able to bear. In the same spirit of gentleness the apostle Paul says a person should never be accelerated into office in the church or into the preaching ministry prematurely. Why not? Because, if a novice, he may fall into the snare of the devil. He needs a little longer in the Christian life, a little more experience of personal spiritual battles, more time to prove the Lord, and to be humbled and strengthened for service.

Hamstring the Horses!

We note that for the northern campaign the special miracles ceased. Those extraordinary demonstrations of God's power such as the crossing of Jordan, the fall of Jericho, the hailstones and the sun standing still, would no longer be seen, but miraculous assistance would certainly continue and the Israelites would secure every victory by divine intervention. The ending of peculiarly spectacular miracles foreshadows what happened when the church of Christ passed from its New Testament foundation stage into the remainder of the Gospel age, at the passing of the apostles. Those initial signs and wonders which authenticated apostles and reproved Jewish unbelief, were soon no more, but miracles of conversion continued, and will do so to the end of the age.

For the northern conquest Israelite problems increased, because now they found themselves contending with cavalry and chariots on a larger scale. They would have to comfort and strengthen themselves with the promises of God and the recollection of past wonders. Today we may see our position as somewhat similar, for we do not see the miracles of earlier times, but we confront a vast population of people brainwashed by scientific humanism, anti-moral ideas, and the pleasures of affluence. Yet the Word of God and the power of the Spirit are sufficient for all things and miracles of conversion are still wrought.

Here, then, is Hazor, the principal mover in this immense coalition. It was a great city, the experts telling us of a population 40-50,000 strong, not counting the many thousands living around the walls. In *Joshua 11.4* we read: 'And they went out, they and all their hosts with them, much people, even as the sand that is upon the sea shore in multitude, with horses and chariots very many.' It was a terrifying company. Normally, these coalition armies would have fought each other, but now they were solidly united against the God of Israel. Once assembled, they marched toward Gilgal and pitched their tents nearby.

'Be not afraid!' was the Lord's word to Joshua, and not for the first time, but now there was a new campaign with a new and dangerous threat, so the divine assurance came again with renewed power. 'Be not afraid because of them: for to morrow about this time will I deliver them up all slain before Israel: thou shalt hough their horses, and burn their chariots with fire.' If Joshua had not listened to the Lord he would surely have found his faith failing, so terrifying were the prospects, but he was sensitive to the voice of God. We do not

(Josh 11.6-9) know in what way God spoke to him but it was in an
unmistakeable way.

In our case, if we do not read the Word, our faith will flounder. We may be confronted in the coming days with a fresh new challenge that we have never encountered before, and if we are not living in the assurance which is built up in us by the Word of God, and by its deep personal devotional study day by day, we will be caught out.

We refer yet again to the crazy things churches are doing today in different parts of the world, trusting in gimmicks and entertainment, as if they have lost their faith in the Word of God alone and the power of the Spirit. One wonders if the inventors of these unbiblical antics ever truly use the Word of God. What has caused their faith to fail so dramatically that they trust in methods of their own making, rather than the Word of God and the power of the Spirit? Strength and assurance will only be channelled to us by God as we focus our minds on His Word. Joshua treasured the words of God, and from them he drew his courage.

He was told to hough or hamstring their horses and burn their chariots with fire. This is partly so that they would not be able to conduct the war as they wished, and partly so that the Israelites would not be tempted to take possession of these horses and chariots in order to use them. God had commanded that horses should not be multiplied by the Israelites. They were to trust in Him, not in cavalry or chariots, and were not to acquire a cavalry capability. A veterinary surgeon once told this writer that what the Israelites did to the horses would not have completely disabled them, leaving them fit for farm work but useless for chariot or cavalry use.

Calvin has a memorable phrase about horses and chariots, saying, 'Showy equipment dazzles the eye and intoxicates the mind with confidence,' and so it does. God did not want them drawing all their optimism and courage from their equipment or from their own skill. He sent them disadvantaged into battle so that they would rely on Him, and the same goes for today. We may use a certain amount of technology for amplification and audio-video reproduction so that the Word may go far and wide, but we do not boast in equipment. We are to resist any temptation to go into the spiritual battle and into soul winning with confidence in either gadgets or humanly devised methods, as if these will somehow make a greater impression than the message earnestly spoken. The Gospel must be everything to us, accompanied by prayer that the Spirit will apply it.

Many years ago a Christian periodical published response figures for the campaign of an international evangelist held in London. The article provided the percentage of mission attenders who professed Christ among the thousands in the main auditorium, and the percentage of professions among those who gathered in hired halls round the country, listening to the preaching by sound-relay. The strange fact emerged that a slightly higher percentage of responses were produced by the relay than by the preacher's voice heard in the auditorium. The writer of the article then seriously urged people to make use of the relays as they were more effective for soul winning.

The organisers of this mission were already trusting in their massive choir, their invitation procedure, and a host of other emotionally manipulative techniques, and now the supposed greater efficacy of relayed sound was to join the list.

Joshua obeyed the prompting of the Lord, attacking the enemy camp 'suddenly' *(Joshua 11.7)*, this being the key word, when the enemy cavalry had not yet mounted, and were possibly still in bed. We may assume the chariots were not prepared nor the horses harnessed. Joshua's troops fell upon them, producing terror in that much larger camp, and the Lord delivered them into the hands of Israel, who chased them a considerable way to salt pits where they were duly defeated. It was not, of course, Joshua's strategy, but the Lord's, for 'Joshua did unto them as the Lord bade him.'

'What are you doing?' some of Joshua's captains might have demanded as the order went out to disable horses and destroy chariots. 'We could do great things with equipment like this.' But by the

Josh 11.9-10 obedience of faith the command of the Lord was carried out.

This sentiment occurs in *Psalm 20.7*: 'Some trust in chariots, and some in horses: but we will remember the name of the Lord our God.' That was the principle taught to Israel, but the princes of Judah did not always honour it, centuries later deserving the rebuke of *Isaiah 31.1*: 'Woe to them that go down to Egypt for help; and stay on horses, and trust in chariots, because they are many; and in horsemen, because they are very strong; but they look not unto the Holy One of Israel, neither seek the Lord!'

In recent times the evangelical world has seen the phenomenal promotion and sales of two books, *The Purpose-driven Church* and *The Purpose-driven Life,* both of which advocate a form of church growth and evangelism that embraces the latest entertainment-idiom music and the shallowest man-centred notion of 'conversion' as the best means of advancing the kingdom of God. The worldwide success of these books, and the number of churches that organise seminars to study them, testifies to the hollowness, even the delusion, of much modern evangelicalism. What is the attraction of the *Purpose-driven* books and seminars? The answer is simple: they are not the Bible; they do not advocate preaching; they do not seek to bring people under conviction of sin; they do not require biblical faith. 'Some trust in chariots, and some in horses.' Any alternative to God's ways will always be attractive to those who lack saving faith or have swerved from their first love.

Another fad now spreads its influence across the Western Christian world, the so-called 'Emerging Church' movement. We read the books of its principal promoters and scarcely find a scripture quoted to justify anything proposed as a means of building and operating churches. Sadly, neglecting biblical authority and disparaging preaching, it is bound to be popular. In the Emerging Church formula, self-interest replaces submission to God; self-expression replaces objective worship; free thinking replaces listening to God, and (once again) entertainment and sensation dislodge reverence. How can its advocates fail to sell books in their millions, for they abandon God's blueprint, and this is exactly what many professing Christians seem to want at the present time.

Such movements as these also flourish by courtesy of deeply compromised 'Christian' publishers, many of which have over the years become huge businesses for maximum profit, often public companies, having no loyalty whatever to the old paths of Truth. If these highly successful commercial publishing companies were not pandering to the declining tastes of modern evangelicals by promoting these books, they would probably have little influence, but now the world of commerce is driving much of the church.

Hazor – the Pivotal Kingdom

Joshua 11.10 makes an intriguing point, for we read that Joshua took particular care to take Hazor first – 'for Hazor beforetime was the head of all those kingdoms'. It was the *key* city-state, the leading one of the coalition, and had to be brought down first as a vital act and a clear signal of victory.

Throughout church history, and especially from the Reformation, defenders of the faith have found it necessary to identify key, pivotal points of error, on which other errors rest, in order to refute them first. There is always a Hazor, a head error of the pack, in any major heresy or error, and if exponents of the Truth can identify this they may effectively refute the wrong and rescue many who are led astray. We think of the Reformation and the doctrine of justification by faith. It was one of five key matters that torpedoed the Roman error and made the Truth clear to many.

In the first place this was Luther's doing. He was a genius at seeing a pivotal issue, the 'city of Hazor' as it were, the key issue to deal with in order to make everything plain. We remember the title of one of his most important works – *The Bondage of the Will*. The title identified the crucial matter in his debate with Erasmus which

Josh 11.12-18 Luther had unerringly located. In our witness we need to do this also. If we are in discussion with someone who is meandering around every imaginable topic between atheism and Christianity, we need to steer to the pivotal matters about the being of God and the way of salvation. It is central to the art of personal witness, as well as the efficiency of preaching, to deal with the head issues – the Hazors.

As far as the northern cities were concerned – 'All the cities of those kings, and all the kings of them, did Joshua take, and smote them with the edge of the sword, and he utterly destroyed them, as Moses the servant of the Lord commanded.' This was not accomplished in a moment, but over a period of years (as verse 18 shows).

In connection with the northern conquest, *Joshua 11.13* is a verse presenting a double problem: 'As for the cities that stood still in their strength, Israel burned none of them, save Hazor only; that did Joshua burn.' What does 'stood still in their strength' mean? The Hebrew means something like this: 'the cities that stood on their mounds'. In other words they were cities which had been built up over many years so that the level of the land had become higher. As buildings had decayed and fallen the bricks and debris became hard core for the new buildings, so the city tended to go up in height. Of the cities that stood high on mounds only Hazor was destroyed by fire.

This does not contradict the record that Jericho and Ai were destroyed by fire also, because *Joshua 11* is speaking only about the northern conquest in which Hazor was the only city burned down. Interestingly, archaeological investigation has shown that Bethel, Debir, Lachish, Eglon, and arguably a number of other cities, were also destroyed by fire, but this does not contradict *Joshua 11* either, because other burnings were probably the work of marauders, such as the sea-peoples. Equally they could have been Egyptian acts of discipline over various rebellions, or the result of inter-city wars. It should not be imagined that Canaan was at peace before the children of Israel came; the opposite was true. Whole cities were often massacred and burned.

The scrupulous obedience of Joshua to God's instructions is again brought out in verse 15 – 'As the Lord commanded Moses his servant, so did Moses command Joshua, and so did Joshua; he left nothing undone of all that the Lord commanded Moses.' The Hebrew literally says – *he removed nothing* of all that the Lord commanded. Neither Moses nor Joshua 'deleted' any of God's instructions, but carried them out to the letter. How much do we remove from the Bible? How many of its commands do we choose to delete, or choose not to apply to our lives or to our church life?

Joshua is quite rightly held up as a type of Christ, because he represents the Lord perfectly in this respect. Our Saviour, when He came, left nothing undone in the work of redemption, but carried out to the letter the plan of God. He came to earth; He accepted great humiliation; He lived a perfect life; He submitted to arrest and brutality; He went to the garden of Gethsemane, then to Calvary, where He bore away the weight of sin for His people. Our Saviour did not leave out a single line of the plan agreed between Himself, the Father and the Holy Spirit in bringing about our salvation. Joshua is certainly a type of Christ.

'So Joshua took,' says verse 16, 'all that land, the hills, and all the south country, and all the land of Goshen, and the valley, and the plain, and the mountain of Israel, and the valley of the same.' Joshua was God's instrument, but it was not this great general and leader who was remembered in the following years, but God. We turn to *Psalm 44* where this is wonderfully put:

'We have heard with our ears, O God, our fathers have told us, what work thou didst in their days, in the times of old. How thou didst drive out the heathen with thy hand, and plantedst them; how thou didst afflict the people, and cast them out. For they *[the Israelites]* got not the land in possession by their own sword, neither did their own arm save them: but thy right hand, and thine arm, and the

(Josh 11.19-20) light of thy countenance, because thou hadst a
favour unto them.'

This was the memory that became embedded in the culture and the teaching of Israel. David the psalmist did not say, 'Was not Joshua a great man and an outstanding general; someone to celebrate?' It was the Lord Who received the honour and glory.

It should concern us that even in fine biographies of great servants of God, which we love to read, the biographer sometimes gets carried away in exalting the human instrument more than the Lord. As Christians we sometimes like to talk about great preachers or some other accomplished servants of God, exaggerating their excellencies somewhat, and in this tendency we lose sight of the fact that we are all 'earthen vessels' and can accomplish nothing of ourselves. As the Gospel is proclaimed, it is by the movement of the Spirit that God accomplishes everything, and we must trust in that and pray for that and not let that vital concept be eroded away.

God's Hardening of Hearts

Perhaps the greatest problem text in these central chapters of *Joshua* is the statement about God hardening the hearts of the Canaanites, found in *Joshua 11.19-20*. It is noted that no city made peace with Israel except Gibeon – 'For it was of the Lord to harden their hearts, that they should come against Israel [as aggressors] in battle, that he might destroy them utterly, and that they might have no favour, but that he might destroy them, as the Lord commanded Moses.'

Does this mean that God was to blame for their obduracy? We have said that Joshua would have offered them peace according to the rules of war given by God, but how could they have chosen peace if the Lord had hardened their hearts? The answer is that the Canaanites on their own account were adamant in their hatred of the God of Israel and His standards, and determined to cling to their lusts and vices, so the Lord then hardened their hearts in order that they would not sue for peace insincerely, out of cunning. If God had not hardened their hearts, these evil city-states may well have surrendered deceitfully, and not like the Gibeonites who really wanted peace. They would have entered into peace while at the same time scheming to overthrow Israel at the first opportunity. Once Israel's forces were spread thinly through the land, and the land was no longer on a war footing, then insurrection would have been initiated.

Without entering into military politics, it seems that this is exactly what happened in Iraq. No sooner had the news media described how the army of Iraq had thrown away its weapons and melted before the invaders, and no sooner had coalition troops become thinly spread through the land, than the insurgency began. The ensuing problem rapidly became worse than the first. Something like this would certainly have taken place in the northern kingdoms, but God prevented this by hardening them in their existing state. They were themselves guilty, saying, in effect, 'We're not going to give way before these Israelites. We will keep our culture and our ways. We're not giving an inch. We hate the God of Israel.' That was their position, and to prevent them pretending to seek peace, God hardened their hearts so that they continued with their aggression, even when it became obvious that the power of God was with the Israelites.

An example of God working in this way appears in *Psalm 81.11-14* in connection with the children of Israel, when they needed to be disciplined. The text reads: 'But my people would not hearken to my voice; and Israel would none of me. So I gave them up unto their own hearts' lust: and they walked in their own counsels. Oh that my people had hearkened unto me, and Israel had walked in my ways! I should soon have subdued their enemies.'

Here is an instance of God hardening the hearts of His own people in order that they should march straight into trouble, be punished, and bring upon themselves the consequences of their godlessness

(Josh 11.20-14.15) and faithlessness. God did not cause their disobedience in the first place, but hardened them in their sin so that they would reap the consequences from corrective discipline.

The same theme is seen in *Romans 1.23-25*. Speaking of the ungodly, it is said that they – 'changed the glory of the uncorruptible God into an image made like to corruptible man, and to birds, and fourfooted beasts, and creeping things. Wherefore *[as the result]* God also gave them up to uncleanness through the lusts of their own hearts, to dishonour their own bodies between themselves: who changed the truth of God into a lie, and worshipped and served the creature more than the Creator, who is blessed for ever.'

Verse 28 continues: 'Even as they did not like to retain God in their knowledge, *[as the result]* God gave them over to a reprobate mind, to do those things which are not convenient.' This is a case of judicial hardening, but the people were entirely responsible for their actions. God was not the author of their sin.

So we go back to *Joshua 11.20*, where the Canaanites were godless, deeply perverted, filled with hate for the God of Israel, and determined to defeat the Israelites. Then God fixed them in that condition so that there could be no subtle, cunning, crafty suing for peace. That is the explanation of these verses.

The Anakim – the Last Enemy

'And at that time came Joshua, and cut off the Anakims from the mountains, from Hebron, from Debir, from Anab, and from all the mountains of Judah, and from all the mountains of Israel: Joshua destroyed them utterly with their cities' *(Joshua 11.21)*.

The last enemies to fall appear to have been the Anakim, the giants of the mountains, from Hebron, Debir, Anab, and elsewhere. Joshua, it is recorded, destroyed them utterly with their cities, and this has great significance. How giant-like they were we cannot tell, although some experts seem to know, speaking of seven to eight feet. We do not know how they know, but it gives our imaginations something to work on.

We have very tall people today but they are mostly long and lean, and we send them to play basketball. The Anakim, however, were clearly as heavy as they were tall. Enormous people would not be so much of a worry in modern warfare, for bullets and bombs are no respecters of size, but in the days of the spear and the sword a giant was formidable. To see thousands of such warriors, far stronger than you are, possessing both power and speed of movement, with tremendous stamina, would strike fear into any opponent. These were the last enemies to fall. Matthew Henry says that it is very significant that in the Christian life the hardest battles are often reserved until the end when faith is at its strongest and experience at its greatest.

We remember the twelve spies sent out by Moses. With the exception only of Joshua and Caleb, these were terrified of the Anakim, and cried out pitifully, 'They are far stronger than we are. There is nothing we can do to withstand them.' Their gloomy report led to the national rebellion just as the Israelites were poised to go into the promised land. Because of fear of the Anakim there followed 38 years of wandering in the wilderness.

Notice who defeated the Anakim. It was the two survivors of the twelve spies, the two who were not afraid of them in the first place. Because they trusted the power of God they were vindicated in the end. Joshua and Caleb were the two, plus a nephew of Caleb, who followed his uncle in faith and valour. Faith's long-term reward was seen, and we see it today not only in Christian families but in Sunday School work. The latter is short-term rewarded and also long-term rewarded. When believers stand at their post while other voices say it is time to give up, they will one day reap the reward of Joshua and Caleb, whose scions helped defeat the last foe. To Caleb was given the main Anakim territory as a final vindication and reward (14.6-15).

Today we have Anakim or giant-like forces against us, such as those already mentioned, the anti-morality crusade of permissiveness and scientific humanism promoted constantly on television and by the press, which is stealing the minds of the masses. Affluence and pleasure-lust also take away the hearts of the people. Every imaginable perversion is available to modern society, and what can we do? The church-growth promoters who trust in human measures say, 'Be as big as the giants! Do things on a huge scale. Find the most exceptional personalities to be your ministers. Recruit the best bands and employ the latest entertainment music. Run with the age. Only mega-churches can take on these giants.'

However, we do not read in *Joshua* that the Israelites were somehow turned into Anakim in order to defeat them. Matthew Henry has a marvellous and well-known saying about the Anakim, which is – 'Giants are dwarfs to omnipotence.' We have the Lord and the power of the Spirit. We have the Word of God. We do not need to be giants in *worldly* accomplishments and capacities to gain spectacular spiritual victories.

The Lord's strategy was proved by Joshua, and will be proved by us today. All the following features of these chapters have some counterpart in our day. The sign miracles are over (just as they subsided then), except for the mighty miracle of salvation in many lives. God's kindness delayed the northern conquest, and still the Lord knows what we can cope with as individual believers, and, if we are earnest for Him, will ration the burdens and trials that we will face in His service and spread them through life. In Joshua's time chariots and horses were not to be used, and we are not to harness gimmicks or rely on human ingenuity. God's strategy had to be obeyed and then His help would be received for every battle, and this is true today. All the credit and glory was the Lord's and was not to be redirected to the glory of human instruments, and so it should be today. The Anakim were the last to fall, and, in our day, people for whom we have prayed all our lives, and obstacles against which we have had to contend all our lives, will fall to gracious conquest in the end. The Lord's strategy must be ours.

6

Truly Believing
Joshua 17 – 20

'Yet the children of Manasseh could not drive out the inhabitants of those cities; but the Canaanites would dwell in that land' *(Joshua 17.12).*

IN *JOSHUA 17.12* we find disturbing words about the tribe of Manasseh. The tribe of Ephraim, for all its self-confidence, had a similar failure, and so did the descendants of Judah, who allowed the Jebusites to remain in Jerusalem. These failings are all about the need for continuing belief in God's commands and promises.

The portions of the land distributed to the tribes are described in chapters 13 to 19, but at the time the distribution was carried out many pagan inhabitants still occupied their territories. Up to this point the Israelites had acted together in overpowering their enemies, but with the apportioning of the land, each tribe would now drive out the remaining Canaanites from its portion. The promise of God was made to the individual tribes just as it had been made to the whole nation – 'them will I drive out from before the

(Josh 15-17) children of Israel' *(Joshua 13.6)*. The inability or unwillingness of the children of Manasseh to drive out the inhabitants of their allotted region introduces a disturbing theme about the breakdown of real belief in God's words. We will be looking here at the phenomenon of people who believe, yet not deeply and fully, a tragic condition which may become true of genuinely converted people in any age.

However, 'the children of Manasseh *could not* drive out the inhabitants of those cities.' This needs a little interpretation because the power of God would have been with them had they tried. The truth is that they *would not* drive out the inhabitants, and they are reproved for this.

Judah's failure is recorded in these words: 'As for the Jebusites the inhabitants of Jerusalem, the children of Judah could not drive them out: but the Jebusites dwell with the children of Judah at Jerusalem unto this day' (15.63).

Ephraim's failure was certainly deliberate, as the Bible says: 'And they drave not out the Canaanites that dwelt in Gezer: but the Canaanites dwell among the Ephraimites unto this day, and serve under tribute' (16.10). Their reluctance to clear the region was obviously wilful, as the king of Gezer and his troops had already been utterly routed by Joshua (10.33), and Ephraim could have made short work of the residue. Obviously the Ephraimites had no intention of driving them out, because they saw that it would be to their advantage to take them into service as labourers. They realised a foreign underclass would greatly help the economy of the region, so they disobeyed the Lord and turned them into servants.

Manasseh did exactly the same thing, disobeying God's warning, which included the words: 'What thing soever I command you, observe to do it: thou shalt not add thereto, nor diminish from it' *(Deuteronomy 12.31-32)*.

The three tribes that failed to drive out the remaining Canaanites in their regions had the authority to do it, the duty to do it, the power to do it (by God's help), and the encouragement of having seen God's power in Joshua's victories, but they would not obey. Why did they choose not to obey the Lord? It may partly have been because they were not prepared to accept losses or endure difficulty. Lack of faith would have caused them to see the task as too demanding. They wanted to settle down in the land, and as soon as they started to farm areas of it and build homes they grew tired of war and were willing to abandon their commission.

However, their faith also failed when they chose not to take seriously God's warnings about the outcome of allowing Canaanites to remain in the land. God's word through Moses was evidently regarded by them as fallible or overstated. Lack of faith soon fathered lack of fear, lack of urgency, and lack of obedience.

'Yet it came to pass, when the children of Israel were waxen strong, that they put the Canaanites to tribute' (17.13). In their lack of true belief they had changed the original vision or policy to suit themselves. They saw there was usefulness in these Canaanites, and this came first.

We can immediately see an application to ourselves, when our true and wholehearted belief wanes, and we feel no urgency to drive out sin from our lives. We may, perhaps, begin to think, 'Is this deed or possession really so offensive to God? Is He really watching us all the time? Will we really be damaged and ensnared, and lose blessing? Are not some worldly recreations and enjoyments pleasant and beneficial? Does God really forbid us participating a little in them?'

When we are first converted there is great fervour on our part, but after a while things sometimes go downhill, so that gradually there is less effort in our spiritual walk. We claim the blessing in prayer (as Ephraim and Manasseh did), but *real* belief, or *deep* belief, has withered. We stick firmly to the fundamentals of salvation, but we begin to disbelieve biblical commands about our lifestyle and service, as well as exhortations to separation and godliness.

Ephraim and Manasseh asked for more territory, pleading their

Josh 17.14 size and strength and blessedness, but the fact was they were not doing what they were supposed to be doing, having changed the whole policy without reference to the Lord. They were using the Canaanites as servants without their submission to Israel's God. How like us! We go on praying, we ask for the help and kindness of God, and yet our effort grows smaller and smaller. We see this in the stance of many reformed evangelical churches today. I am sorry to have to make this comment, but how few Bible and ministers' conferences, among the many that take place, are about evangelism! How few are about Sunday School labours! How few are about personal witness, and how to be more effective! Driving the Canaanites out of the land for Christ seems to have gone out of our reckoning and out of our policy, but we continue to be sure that we are believing Christians. The truth is we have largely stopped believing the scriptures that tell us that these ministries are our highest responsibility. Like the failing tribes, instead of fighting against worldliness, we bring the world into our homes and into our churches. The record of *Joshua* is literal history, but it is recorded for our admonition and learning, and these applicatory parallels are immensely important.

We notice that when the Israelites were fighting as one nation under Joshua, they pulled their weight, but as soon as the tribes were given their own land with a mission to clear it, all the spirit and fight and enthusiasm seemed to go out of them. Sometimes it is the same with us. When we are working together with others in the congregation we can do great things and accomplish extensive projects, but as soon as we go back to our individual service for Christ the effort disappears (especially in striving to witness).

All this is ultimately a belief problem. We believe in the Lord, and have proved Him in the past, but somehow the Word has become less real, less encouraging, less stirring, and less threatening. So the conscientious believer becomes unwatchful, unconcerned about the details of life, seldom repenting of besetting sins, and uncaring of his bad stewardship of time, so that the habits of the old, unregenerate life slowly return. The old unkindness, selfishness, laziness, and self-consideration creep back into life, and these traits are not fought any more. The Word no longer challenges backsliding and hypocrisy, because the Word is no longer believed quite as deeply as it used to be. It is imperative that we pull ourselves together and return to *believing* Christian living, or we shall decline. After the death of Joshua and his surviving elders, the land declined so badly that the terrible situation recorded in the last chapters of *Judges* came to pass, and the entire nation became depraved, decadent and backslidden to a horrific degree.

The Failure of Effort

The 'prayer' or request made to Joshua by Manasseh and Ephraim was: 'Why hast thou given me but one lot and one portion to inherit, seeing I am a great people, forasmuch as the Lord hath blessed me hitherto?' (17.14.) Their view of their situation was not right, because they had two lots. Were they being dishonest? Not quite, for they really meant to say, 'Oh, Joshua, one lot is good, but the other is covered in trees and occupied by Canaanites.' Although they had been given the 'other' lot with the command to drive out the occupants, they did not want to drive them out, so in their minds this lot was untenable and nonexistent.

The land was the gift of God, but there were certain things they had to do to honour and adorn it, and similarly there are things we have to do today. By grace we have redemption through the blood of Christ, our sins washed away, a new nature, new life, and fellowship with God, but we have a part to play in clearing the territory, and God will enable us if we only try. We have to be active in ongoing sanctification. The people of Manasseh and Ephraim had one excellent lot, and a second which needed to be cleared. Matthew Henry commented long ago that there are many Christians who, like those tribes, want greater benefits when they have not made the

Josh 17.15-18.3   best of those that they have.

Joshua's response is to expose their pride, feebleness and lack of vision in a single stroke, saying – 'If thou be a great people, then get thee up to the wood country, and cut down for thyself there in the land of the Perizzites and of the giants, if mount Ephraim be too narrow for thee' (verse 15). They are bluntly told to clear the ground and expel the people from the rest of the territory. Joshua appears to have little sympathy for them. They, however, continue to complain, saying, 'The hill is not enough for us: and all the Canaanites that dwell in the land of the valley have chariots of iron . . .'

'But you do not understand,' they seem to be saying to Joshua, 'we are a great people, but you are setting us an impossible and unreasonable task. These Canaanites have far superior equipment, and to drive them out would be grievously costly, if not impossible.' The truth was, they had no *deep* belief either in God's commands or His power to see them through. Chariots of iron had been overcome before in the battle against the Hazor coalition when the Israelites faced far, far greater numbers. Manasseh and Ephraim were simply unwilling and fearful, but strangely, this did not shake their self-belief.

The lesson is that self-belief soon supplants belief in God, and so it does with us. As self-confidence rises, real faith diminishes, and proving of the Lord comes to a halt. Self-approval in any matter will always reduce dependence on the Lord and trust in His promises and power. Sometimes pride will increase to the point of absurdity, as it did with those two self-deluded tribes who said, 'Look how God has blessed us, and see how great and numerous we are.'

What does Joshua have to say about their continued protest? He effectively repeats exactly the same message as before, this time challenging them to demonstrate their boasted greatness by action. 'Joshua spake unto the house of Joseph, even to Ephraim and to Manasseh, saying, Thou art a great people, and hast great power:

thou shalt not have one lot only: but the mountain shall be thine; for it is a wood, and thou shalt cut it down: and the outgoings of it shall be thine [ie: the entire territory as far as you can go]: for thou shalt drive out the Canaanites, though they have iron chariots, and though they be strong.'

The commands of God do not change, and Joshua spells out their duties. Like a judge in his summing-up he sets out their case and its resolution. 'You tell me that you are great; you say you occupy only one assigned piece of land; well then, the neighbouring portion that you have disdained will be yours, and you will expel the Canaanites in spite of their iron chariots and great strength.' God does not change His orders because we fail to trust Him. If we pray to Him for a smoother, easier passage and exemption from the rigours of holiness His answer will only be to reaffirm His commands to mortify sin, witness for Him and serve Him. In these things alone will we find triumph and delight.

We may pray, 'Lord, I need this, I need that. I need more assurance. I must have . . .' The Lord says, as He said through Joshua, 'You have spiritual life; you have much blessing; now get down to devotions and Bible study, and serve Me with all your heart.' This is the way to live the spiritual life. So we must go forward in sanctification and service, attending the means of grace whenever we possibly can, not just now and then. We must return to regular prayer meeting attendance, apply ourselves to the defence of the faith and renewed efforts of fellowship among the Lord's people. This will be our way of cutting down the forest and the wood, expelling the Canaanites, and possessing the blessing.

The Lord's answer through Joshua is in our best interests, for He is a sympathetic and kind Lord beyond all our imagination, but He insists that those trees are cut down, the ground cleared, and the Canaanites driven out. His rules will not change because we want to do it some other way. These are the kind of lessons we learn, but unfortunately the children of Israel were very slow to learn them, and at length Joshua would say to them, 'How long are ye slack to go to possess the land, which the Lord God of your fathers hath given you?' *(Joshua 18.3.)*

The Cities of Refuge

Our chapter heading is 'Truly Believing', and this perfectly suits the remarkable and fascinating instruction of Joshua to implement the Lord's provision of 'cities of refuge'. All this is in

(Josh 20)

Joshua 20. These cities of refuge would be places of safety for people who had committed 'casual murder' – a term coined in the sixteenth century to describe accidental murder. This could easily occur, but the hapless accidental murderer would then fall prey to an ugly and deep-seated habit in the ancient world, namely, that the nearest relation would take vengeance. This idea of a life for a life irrespective of circumstances was not part of God's ordinance, but vengeance was allowed to them for the time being, and the Lord provided alongside it a just solution for the innocent 'killers' by means of cities of refuge. The people in those times were very attached to the law of vengeance, but it could go badly wrong, because in the heat of the moment the next of kin might not know that the death had come about by accident. That relation would then take a posse or group of elders or people from the village or township, and off they would go to seize and kill the offender.

Six cities of refuge were appointed in strategic positions to serve the whole nation *(Numbers 35.6, 11, 14)*, three on either side of the Jordan. The roads to each would be well kept, and elders of communities in the regions through which such roads passed would have to go out and repair the bridges annually.

Deuteronomy 19 gives an example of an innocent killing, describing the plight of a man who enters a copse with his neighbour to cut wood, and, as he wields his axe, the head flies off and kills his neighbour. Such a man may take recourse to the nearest city of refuge. Why is this provision for refuge spoken about so much, and why are the regulations given in such detail? Obviously it is an important arrangement, but it is also intended as a picture of Christ and of the mercy of salvation, like so many other Old Testament provisions.

Before we show how this is so, we must allay the fears of readers who feel uncomfortable about seeing typical parallels in the Old Testament. Here are three proofs that the cities of refuge were intended to serve as a picture of redemption. First, their spiritual significance is evident from the fact that these cities were specifically given to the tribe of Levi and to the priests to keep. They were all priestly cities (named as such in *Joshua 21*), indicating that there was a religious, ceremonial purpose to them as well as a judicial purpose, that purpose being to foreshadow Christ. Secondly, the Lord uses the figure of a refuge for Himself, this being one of the great terms for Him in the Old Testament. 'The eternal God is thy *refuge*' says *Deuteronomy 33.27*, and numerous psalms echo the sentiment, such as 'God is our refuge *[place of shelter]* and strength' *(Psalm 46.1).*[*] This is the Lord's own term for His saving kindness.

Thirdly, there is also a clear indication of the symbolic, typical purpose of these cities in *Hebrews 6*, to which we will refer shortly.

Under the rules, if an accidental killer pursued by avengers could only reach the very edge of the city suburbs, or the outer fields where the cattle grazed, he would be safe. Once the fugitive reached the city gates, the elders would hear his plea, and he would be entitled to refuge until an arrangement could be made for a proper trial. If he were found guilty, he would obviously be dealt with according to the law; but if innocent, he would live out his life in the care of that city. Only when the officiating high priest for the time died would he be allowed to return to the town or village from where he came under the protection of the law of Israel, and his avenger would not be allowed to touch him without incurring the death

---

[*] Other examples: *2 Samuel 22.3; Psalm 9.9; 14.6; 48.3; 57.1; 59.16; 62.7-8; 91.2, 9; 94.22; 142.5;* plus references in the prophets.

(Josh 20) penalty himself. These were the arrangements for cities of refuge. It is said that wherever you were in the land, there was a city of refuge not more than a half-day's travel away.

As an illustration of the mercy of God through the Lord Jesus Christ the cities of refuge provide this message. *He* is the city of refuge for sinners, and if we will only get under the shadow of Calvary, trusting in what He has done, and yielding our life into His hands, we will be safe. If we trust in the atoning work of Christ, condemnation can never seize us; eternal death can never take us. This city of refuge is not far away, and is easily reached from wherever we are. The roads are kept clear, because God's ear is always open to seeking prayer, and Christ is always accessible to those convicted by sin and fearing for their eternal destiny.

The operative word in the provision of cities of refuge is 'flee', mentioned three times in chapter 20 (and used repeatedly in other references also). The word implies 'vanish', or run like the wind. You had to move. A terrible accident has occurred; the next of kin has raised a posse; they are coming with spears and bows and arrows, and the offender had better move quickly. What a picture! As a depiction of salvation it tells us we cannot just stroll along because this will lead to us being overtaken by pursuing temptation and drawn back into the world. Seeking Christ is seen here as a journey having dangers and demanding great urgency.

Can I come to Christ in a very relaxed way? Is it fitting to say, 'Well, I think I'll try this out. Maybe it would be nice to have some blessing from God. I like the idea of forgiveness and Heaven, so perhaps I will get round to asking for it.' The cities of refuge show that is no way to approach Christ. We come to Him when there is a deep concern within us, which says, 'I am going to hell, and I deserve to go there; I'm under the judgement of God; I have sinned against Him; I cannot live without His pardon and forgiveness. The enemy of my soul is tempting me, pursuing me; I'm being chased by my sin, by judgement and guilt, and by the enemy of souls. I will run to

Christ to get under His protection, under His shadow.'

The refugee ran to the city of refuge with all his might, the thundering of horses' hooves not far behind him. He did not pause for anything or see any other matter as more important.

At this point we turn to *Hebrews 6.18* where the inspired writer uses these words about believers: '. . . we might have a strong consolation, WHO HAVE FLED FOR REFUGE TO LAY HOLD ON THE HOPE set before us.' That phrase 'have fled for refuge' is without any question a reference back to the cities of refuge. This, remember, is a letter to Hebrew Christians, converted Jews, deeply taught in all their traditions and ways, and here the writer picks up this illustration from the cities of refuge, making no attempt to explain it, probably because it was a popular theme with Jewish converts.

Christians are those who have *fled for refuge*. By the operation of the Spirit in our hearts, and deeply affected by God's Word, we became concerned about our sin, knowing we deserved to die. Desperate to find the Lord, we ran to Him. We realised that if we believed in Him and pressed to get within the shadow of Calvary, we would be safe. And so it was, for our guilt was taken away, we were reconciled with God, and the condemnation which pursued us down life's journey, pulled back, unable to reach us.

Charles Wesley, in one of his greatest hymns, 'Jesus, lover of my soul,' ranges through a wide variety of figures from the haven sheltering vessels from fierce seas, to the rock at Horeb, referring *en route* to the cities of refuge[*] in these words:–

> *Other refuge have I none;*
> *Hangs my helpless soul on Thee;*
> *Leave, ah! leave me not alone,*
> *Still support and comfort me:*
> *All my trust on Thee is stayed;*
> *All my help from Thee I bring;*
> *Cover my defenceless head*
> *With the shadow of Thy wing.*

---

[*] Via *Psalm 57.1* uniting the refuge figure of the cities with that of the horns of the altar.

(Josh 20)   Remarkably, under the rules, the refugee who reached a city of refuge had everything provided for him. He did not have to work (so some of the old commentators say), or lift a finger to contribute to his maintenance. The priests must care for him. He did not own a homestead there, and would live at the charge of the community. No doubt out of goodwill he would have contributed some effort, but the rules of refuge asked for none.

Similarly, in salvation, if we get to the kingdom of Christ, to the eternal city of refuge, everything we need is provided for us. We receive new life, and all the kindness of the Lord in wonderful things such as answered prayer, communion with Himself, fellowship with His people on earth, and joy, peace and assurance. Our souls are fed from the royal table. The cities of refuge yield up a beautiful picture and their rules speak of the promise of mercy through Christ.

There is yet more counsel for seekers in this picture. You are on the run to the city of refuge, so what will you do? Will you pause every so often and say, 'Oh, that's a nice field over there, I'll go and look at it. That's a nice little wood, I'll go and explore. There is a wonderful view from this hilltop; I have never seen a view like this, so I'll sit down and survey it for a while'? You would not dare! You are being chased and your life is in the balance. You must keep your lead at all costs, even if you are becoming exhausted.

It is just like this when you are seeking Christ. You dare not say, 'I feel a need of Him today, but tomorrow I'll go somewhere else, and do something else, and then return to the matter of my soul at some later time. I'll spend a few days pursuing some new hobby, and getting excited about something quite different.' You dare not do that! If you did, the urgency and the need would just vanish from your head, and the devil would pursue you and drag you back more deeply than ever into the love of this world. The whole idea of a pursuit to the city of refuge illustrates the dangers of deviation and distraction.

One more rule for the cities of refuge also pictures Christ, for we read concerning the refugee (20.6) – 'And he shall dwell in that city, until he stand before the congregation for judgment, and until the death of the high priest that shall be in those days.' Why ever is this said? Why would the refugee have hospitality in the city of refuge until the currently serving high priest died, and on his death be free to return to his home without a stain on his character? There is no conceivable reason why the death of the high priest should be the point at which he were set free, unless this were intended to picture the death of the great High Priest, Jesus Christ, through which we are all ultimately set free, and by Whom we receive salvation.

The following observation on the cities of refuge gives us insight into how we should conduct ourselves in the church of Christ. The Israelites had to keep the roads to the cities clear, and we also have to do that in our preaching and witness. When a minister presents an evangelistic sermon it may involve all kinds of reasoning and exhortation, but the supreme matter is that the road to the city of refuge must be clear, and Christ must be seen. If we speak to children in Sunday School classes or we have a visiting speaker to address the Sunday School anniversary, the road to the city of refuge must be clear. The message could be wonderful, but souls cannot be saved if the road to the city of salvation is tortuous or obstructed.

Every evangelistic sermon or address must lead directly and clearly to Calvary, to the Cross of Christ and the way of redemption. I hope as a preacher of the Gospel never to hear the complaint after an evangelistic sermon, 'Pastor, the road to the city of refuge was obscured tonight.' Nothing is more vital than that we keep the Gospel clear and accessible to everyone, and open to adults and children alike. A final observation from this great figure is about the exercise of faith.

The cities of refuge are all about truly believing. Without real belief in the security of those cities would anyone run for up to half a day, heart pounding, assailants in pursuit? Would it not be better to hide somewhere nearby in the hope that somehow he would survive? Just as belief in that city is essential to the refugee, so also the seeker after Christ must truly believe His promise – 'Him that cometh to me I will in no wise cast out.'

True believing is the goal for long established Christians also. If we have been saved by God, are we also truly believing in the necessity of a sanctified life and service for the Lord? Are we convinced this and this alone is the pathway of blessing? Do we really believe that God sees us day by day, and observes what we are doing and how we are speaking and how we are behaving? Do we truly believe He scans our thoughts and is deeply concerned about the state of our minds? Are we really convinced He will reprove and chastise us if we backslide, or bless us if we seek His help to advance? If we really believe in our Lord as Christians, we will be concerned to win the territory of our lives, just as the ancients had to drive the Canaanites out of their land. Let us never say, 'But I do believe,' if we do not believe enough to run; if we do not believe enough to fear; if we do not believe enough to want to please the Lord.

7
Loyalty and Accountability
Joshua 22 – 24

'Then Joshua called the Reubenites, and the Gadites, and the half tribe of Manasseh, and said unto them . . . Ye have not left your brethren these many days unto this day, but have kept the charge of the commandment of the Lord your God. And now the Lord your God hath given rest unto your brethren, as he promised them: therefore now return ye, and get you unto your tents, and unto the land of your possession . . .' (Joshua 22.1-4).

WE COME TO THE POINT here where Joshua sends home the tribes who had settled on the east of Jordan, and yet had come across to the west with the others to join them in their battles to purge the land. These tribes had solemnly promised Moses they would fight alongside the others, and this they had done. They had been with the main body of the children of Israel for over seven years at this point, a very long time, and had patiently served until the Conquest was complete. They did not seem to be agitating to return and settle in their homes, dearly as they wanted to go, but they waited for Joshua's command. They were absolutely loyal, waiting to be dismissed.

The easterners clearly did not see themselves as free agents, and

Josh 22.1-5 this is a fine example to present-day believers. While there is much liberty for the children of God, we must recognise we should be stable and loyal in the Lord's service and stick at things. We should never uproot lightly or abandon avenues of service and duties which are obviously necessary, and where our loss would injure or strain the work.

To be anecdotal, we encountered this at the Metropolitan Tabernacle some thirty to thirty-five years ago when the work was building up from a very low point. There was a tendency for some of the new younger people, who had found the Lord, or come to a deeper faith, including students and nurses, to have wandering ways. They were excellent people who wanted to come to the Tabernacle and identify in every way, but they were not regularly here because their inclination was to visit other churches whenever a relative had a birthday, or a friend elsewhere was being baptised. For all sorts of events and reasons they would be gone. Whenever the urge took them, or they were curious about something somewhere, off they went. And so they spent only a percentage of their time at the church they genuinely wanted to be their home church.

Had this continued, as it has done in many churches, it would have certainly led to the continued impoverishment and disintegration of the work. Our 'mission' would have been unworkable, and the newly rebuilt Sunday School could never have been staffed, nor any other activity of the church to win souls sustained. So, naturally, we appealed to the young to recognise the preciousness and duty of consistency and loyalty, and they did so, and responded wholeheartedly. So the practice formed for people to be very loyal, going away only when on holiday or when it was really necessary. No rules were made and no one was 'monitored', but the value of commitment was freely recognised and honoured. Casual invitations by distant friends to rush off and visit were treated far more circumspectly.

We sought as a church to honour the spirit of the Keach covenant, which has been the basis of fellowship at the Tabernacle for generations going back to the seventeenth century, and which stresses reliability in service. The result is that we have been able to build up every department of the work because teachers and helpers have not been absent one or two weeks out of three, and we have been able to move ahead wonderfully and prove the blessing of the Lord in so many ways. Incidentally, this is what all churches used to be like before the last forty or so years when wanderlust seems to have become a basic human right and a necessity.

The two-and-a-half tribes stood by their pledge and duty tirelessly and patiently for seven years, undertaking all that was required of them until Joshua was led of God to tell them it was time to go home.

Duties of Law and Love

As they prepared to return, Joshua's parting command was that they should take great pain – 'to do the commandment and the law, which Moses the servant of the Lord charged you'. This phrase is very arresting – 'the commandment and the law'. A distinction is probably intended between the moral law of the Ten Commandments and all the other commandments, which were for the government of state and for ceremonial (or teaching) purposes. The word 'keep' in Hebrew has the idea of 'guard' and so they are to be careful to keep all the laws safe and intact.

We have several layers of law to think about today. As Christians we are still under the moral law of God. It does not save us because we cannot keep it adequately to be accepted by God. We are saved only by Christ's suffering and death on Calvary, when He took the punishment due to us for our sin. But as saved people we have a binding commitment and duty to keep the moral law of the Ten Commandments. In addition we have other laws or rules to keep, defining the lifestyle of the Christian. We are, for instance, to read the Word and pray; to conduct ourselves always in a fitting manner; and to promote the Gospel, the Word of God. Other lifestyle rules

Josh 22.5-12 include keeping ourselves clear from, or separate from, the sins and distinctive habits of the world. So we have 'layers' of law, just as they had in 'the commandments and the law'.

Joshua's charge to the eastern tribes continues with the simple but profound words – 'to love the Lord your God'. To love the Lord is to appreciate Him intelligently, to be ever learning more about Him, to desire Him, to speak to Him constantly and to obey Him. As believers today we have so much light, and we are to love Him especially for Calvary and salvation.

Then we must be careful to love Him not only for what He has done for us in salvation, but also for Who He is, and this is vital. Although precious, it is not enough to love Him for His provisions, but increasingly as we go along the Christian pathway we are to love Him for Who He is: His great being; the triune character of God, His attributes, His plans, and especially the characteristics of the eternal Son revealed for us.

We know about this very well in human friendship and love. We do not only love or like a person for what that person may do for us, but for what that person is, and so we must learn of Christ, and love and praise and worship Him. He is a barren and sickly Christian who has barely met and seen his Lord.

Joshua further commands them to 'love the Lord your God, and to walk in all his ways'. That is, they are to conduct themselves constantly and progressively in the rules of life for God's children. They are also to 'cleave unto him', to stick to Him, implying that many forces will conspire to shake their loyalty and draw them away. The only way to maintain loyalty, says Joshua, is to 'serve him with all your heart and with all your soul'. When ardour and earnestness grow cold, then the mind opens to Satan's suggestions, worldly allurements and self-indulgent desires. We can distinguish between *heart* and *soul* in Joshua's exhortation. The two words refer to serving God with all our human faculties, and also serving Him with our spiritual faculty, or soul, in prayer and worship. These are the two distinctive parts of service for the Lord.

So the eastern tribes were blessed and sent away with approval, being given their due share of the spoils of battle, including silver, gold, brass and iron, and they departed. But what came next in the record of their journey was entirely unexpected and baffling, constituting one of the strangest events in the story of Israel.

The Entry of 'Tokenism' and Theatre

The men of Reuben and Gad, with the contingent of Manasseh, were heading out of Canaan for Gilead where they were settled, when their leaders decided a memorial should be built. On the west bank of the Jordan, near where they would cross, they constructed a gigantic altar, probably a replica of that in the Tabernacle pitched at Shiloh. It was very large, to attract the attention of passers-by, and designed to be a showpiece. It turned out they never intended to use it, which was just as well because that would have been an extreme offence against the commandments of the Lord. They built it not to be practical but to be a huge symbol that the tribes east of Jordan were the same as the western tribes, and members of the same nation.

However, it nearly brought about civil war because they do not seem to have told Joshua, Eleazar or anyone else what they were going to do. This suggests that they acted on impulse, responding without much reflection to someone's 'good idea' when they found themselves at Jordan. As soon as the word filtered back to the other tribes it caused tremendous commotion. 'These people, what have they done?' was the reaction, in so many words. They 'have built an altar over against the land of Canaan, in the borders of Jordan.'

Princes and representatives of all the tribes and great families held an emergency assembly at Shiloh, with the realisation that war would be unavoidable if the eastern tribes did not repent and demolish their altar. Their altar was sinful because it repudiated the

(Josh 22.13-30) law of God and gave birth to a new idolatry. It also shattered the unity of the nation. Without punishment in accordance with the Lord's commands, judgement would fall on the whole of Israel.

The eastern tribes, it seemed, had committed a shocking crime, judged in the light of God's commission to the nation – 'Ye shall utterly destroy all the places, wherein the nations which ye shall possess served their gods, upon the high mountains, and upon the hills . . . and ye shall overthrow their altars, and break their pillars, and burn their groves' *(Deuteronomy 12.2-3)*.

All rival altars had to be destroyed. In that same chapter of *Deuteronomy* the clear instruction was given to Israel about the one altar that God would permit: 'But when ye go over Jordan, and dwell in the land which the Lord your God giveth you to inherit, and when he giveth you rest from all your enemies round about, so that ye dwell in safety; then there shall be a place which the Lord your God shall choose to cause his name to dwell there; thither shall ye bring all that I command you; your burnt offerings, and your sacrifices, your tithes . . . and all your choice vows.' This command is repeated, and coupled with a specific prohibition of any other altar in any other place in the land.

There would only be one Tabernacle, and in due course, one Temple replacing it. The command is emphatic that there must be only one focal point for the worship of the people, where God would meet with them. There would be one nation, one faith, one God, and one place where He would meet them and reveal Himself to them. There would be one source of authority, just as today we insist there is one Word of God. We are many different congregations, but we have only one legitimate authority, the Word of God, and like the one altar of olden times, this must never be challenged.

The assembly of Shiloh *(Joshua 22.13)* sent to the eastern tribes a solemn delegation representing all the western tribes, consisting of princes led by Phinehas. These charged the easterners with the grotesque sin of building a rival altar, rebelling against the Lord, and bringing judgement and disaster upon the nation. By building it, were they not saying they were independent and free to do as they pleased, repudiating the revelation of God? Why had they done this? Was this not once again the iniquity of Peor (verse 17), when in early days the children of Israel had compromised by sacrificing to Moabite gods? Would it not bring down the same judgement of God they experienced then? Had they so soon forgotten Achan when everyone had to suffer because of the crime of one?

So serious was the manner of Phinehas (and rightly so), that it seemed to the easterners like a formal notice of war rather than a call to repent.

On being challenged and charged in this way the leaders of the eastern tribes were horrified, because they had never intended to commit the offences now laid before them. 'If what you say is true,' they said, 'we deserve your judgement and God's, but we never built this altar for worship and offerings, nor as an expression of rebellion.' The giant symbol, they explained, arose from a fear of separation. As they faced the Jordan they began to worry about the long-term effect of this barrier of water dividing the territories. They saw in their minds a day when a new generation of westerners would think they were not part of the nation of Israel, for they were not strictly resident in the promised land. This new generation would not remember that the easterners spent seven sacrificial years in the west, fighting their battles with them, and they would say Jordan was the border, and the easterners were enemies.

So, said the easterners, they had reproduced the altar at Shiloh as a symbol of the fact that they were of the same land. There it would stand at the customary crossing point, declaring that east of Jordan was not a different land or territory, but tribes of Israel, loyal to the altar at Shiloh.

Phinehas and the elders of Israel were delighted to hear this. It was not a great sin that was being committed after all; the altar was just

(Josh 22) an enormous symbol of unity. The easterners had no intention of offering sacrifices there. To Phinehas and the princes it seemed as though God's certain judgement had been withdrawn already, and in due course, the whole land would hear the news and be equally relieved and happy.

However, this remarkable episode is recorded to make us think, and to draw a significant application for the life of the church today. The outcome was good, and the easterners were not guilty of the terrible crime of apostasy, but there is no doubt they should never have engaged in this absurdly theatrical monument at all. It seemed a good idea, but it nearly caused a civil war. It seemed a good idea, but it had not been commanded. Moses had never mentioned such a project, and the constant emphasis of *Joshua* is that everything should be done exactly as Moses had instructed.

This altar had not even been discussed with Joshua and Eleazar before the easterners left Shiloh, for they knew nothing about it. It seemed a good idea, but it had no foundation in God's will and purpose. (Are not Bible-believing churches today assailed with bright ideas that have no justification or example in the Word of God?)

In reality it was not a good idea, but a disastrous one for several reasons, any of which should have been seen by the eastern leaders, men of undoubted stature, and would have been if they had taken time to consider. Firstly, their project was bound to be misunderstood, which is exactly what happened. The westerners thought they were in rebellion, acting independently, blaspheming and profaning the true altar of God.

Secondly, their huge altar could so easily have been subverted, and probably was in the course of time. An unused altar would sooner or later be utilised by a wayward Israelite or a Canaanite. Someone would be drawn into sin, if not a considerable portion of the nation. It was asking for trouble.

Thirdly, it would set a precedent in Israel for unofficial, unprescribed projects supposedly promoting the religious and national life of Israel. Superfluous good ideas would soon fog and obscure the divinely appointed symbolism of their worship and life, especially if the additions were much bigger than the originals, as in the case of this outsized altar.

Fourthly, this human initiative would draw the attention of the people away from the perfectly adequate provisions God had already made to solve the problem they feared. In other words, it was utterly unnecessary to build their huge altar. Were not the arrangements put in hand by Moses enough? Was not the Word of God sufficient for their difficulty?

The problem that exercised the easterners was the dividing influence of Jordan. Why did they assume that Moses had not provided for this possibility already? Why did they think (and this was unprecedented) that they would have to concoct a solution of their own? The Word of God through Moses was wholly sufficient. If it had not provided a special device for trans-Jordan unity, then they should have concluded none was necessary, and not have decided that God had forgotten about them.

In the event God had provided antidotes to isolation, commanding that the eastern tribes would go to Shiloh on pilgrimage, so there would have been huge numbers of representatives in the worshipping capital of the west, probably several times a year. Such visitors would have been recognised and related to, and a great sense of oneness would have been enjoyed in Shiloh at these times.

Furthermore, Moses had laid down (from the Lord) that the people must teach the history of the nation to generation after generation, and the youngsters must learn about Jordan, the Conquest, and the settlement of the portions of land. They must hear about the sacrificial service for seven years given by the easterners to the westerners, because the teachers were to make certain that everyone knew about these things.

Also, the representatives of families and the princes of the eastern tribes would attend the great councils of Israel whenever they were

Josh 22-23.3 called. It was utterly unnecessary to build this outsized altar, which would, in any case, itself need to be explained to each new generation.

Soon after my conversion as a late teenager, some of the adults in the church I attended formed the opinion that there was not enough fellowship, and they pressed the officers for a Saturday evening social to be held once a month. The church was in spiritual decline, and things they would never have done in earlier years were coming in. They had in mind a mild sort of party where they would have games and fun and laughter, and they really thought this would solve the problem.

Looking on as a youngster, I remember a silver-haired deacon insisting that they did not need a social. 'All we have to do to solve this problem,' he pointed out, 'is to talk to each other.' A social, he maintained, would not achieve that. It was as though they wanted more fellowship but were too lazy to talk to each other, so they tried to devise an alternative and, to their taste, a more enjoyable (and juvenile) activity.

The same temptation still appears today in some shape or form. A believer wants to know more Christians, so he organises a party in his garden. Why not just talk to other people? Why not engage in an avenue of Christian service alongside them? What could possibly be better than that? Why did the eastern Israelites build an enlarged replica of the altar when there was excellent 'machinery' already in hand to maintain the unity of the tribes?

The easterners were afraid of drifting apart, so they built a monument, something showy, something that could be seen. It was mere tokenism, sentimentality, or theatre. Churches today may wonder how they might decorate the front interior of the sanctuary. Would it not be a good idea to have a large cross positioned high above the pulpit to remind everyone that they are a Christian church? But do they not preach Christ and Calvary clearly and with conviction every week? Is this not a far superior way, and more honouring to Christ, than mere tokenism or symbolism?

There are endless examples of tokenism or theatre in our churches today, so many that we could be seen as intellectual descendants of the eastern tribes. Countless good ideas creep in, sentimental embellishments and token symbolism. The so-called Emerging Church movement, referred to already, builds numerous 'altars', proliferating extra-biblical symbols as worship 'props', and any other 'good idea' anyone may propose as long as it is not in the fusty old Bible.

The point is that the Word of God is always sufficient, because in it God has provided for all our needs and prescribed all the methods for the conduct of His work, and His worship, and we should keep away from human additions, which really say that the Word is not good enough. The grand old Reformation and Puritan principle holds good in every age: the belief in Scripture alone, as our all-sufficient and sole authority as Christians.

The Greater Accountability of Churches

'And it came to pass a long time after that the Lord had given rest unto Israel from all their enemies round about, that Joshua waxed old and stricken in age' *(Joshua 23.1)*. (Josh 23)

Between chapters 22 and 23 lies at least twenty years of unrecorded history. The aged Joshua (he would die at 110 years of age) now calls his last great convocation of the princes, judges and officers of Israel to give his final instructions, together with promises from God and warnings against apostasy. As he begins his counsels, he points to their remarkable experiences and faces them with their responsibility. 'Ye have seen all that the Lord your God hath done unto all these nations because of you.' 'You have seen things,' he says, 'and that makes you accountable. You have had unique privileges, and seen great miracles far beyond anything which most people will see in all their lives. You have seen nations humbled to your advantage, and you have received your portions of land. You, of all people, have a binding responsibility to love Him and to cleave

Josh 23.3-16) to Him.' That is Joshua's reasoning. Obedience and love and purity in religion will be vital.

We may apply this same reasoning to ourselves in these last days. We have been converted. We have known the grace of God, and felt His power in our lives. We have received wonderful answers to our prayers. We have sometimes seen astonishing tokens of God's grace and power, and we are therefore all the more accountable for our privileges, and have a greater obligation to love Him and serve Him faithfully. The challenge of Joshua rings in our ears today – 'Ye have seen . . . !'

In these words, there is also a rousing plea to those who have heard the Gospel many times and are still unconverted. You have heard the Gospel, and have seen how it has changed the lives of other people. At times this has gripped your heart and you have seen very vividly your own need of Christ. You have sometimes wanted Him and longed to find Him, and you have been sure that the Gospel is true. You must realise that you are all the more responsible because of what you have seen and understood. You are not a person still in complete darkness about the needs of the soul, and unaware of Christ and what He has done to bring salvation. You have heard these things many times, and you are therefore all the more accountable should you turn away in the end and reject Christ. This is the challenge of Joshua's words.

The exhortation in verse 6 is so relevant for today: 'Be ye therefore very courageous to keep and to do all that is written in the book of the law of Moses, that ye turn not aside therefrom to the right hand or to the left.' The Hebrew word here translated 'courageous' essentially means very strong; however, it is not applied to fighting but to guarding and preserving all the moral and lifestyle duties of the Word. But why would they require strength? Because there would be great pressure, Joshua implies, from both the right hand and the left, to swerve aside. He immediately specifies the source of these pressures, namely their neighbours the Canaanites. There will be powerful temptations to adopt their ways, their luxuries, their behaviour, their culture, and, worst of all, their idols. You must not look, says Joshua, to the nation on your left or the nation on your right, but cleave (literally 'stick') to the Lord, His standards, His purposes and His ways. God has driven out these nations, great and strong as they were, and none of them has been able to resist. 'One man of you shall chase a thousand', your strength by God's help will be so great.

So it has been with us, for at conversion God drove out powerful sins and character traits that had dominion or mastery over us, and subsequently has helped us to defeat them. But if we begin to look with interest and desire at the world around us, we will soon succumb to its ways and admire its idols, becoming subject once again to the very things that God drove out of us in the miracle of conversion.

The Power of Love Over Backsliding

How may we fortify ourselves to resist the return of old sins? Joshua supplies the perfect antidote in these words: 'Take good heed therefore unto yourselves, *that ye love the Lord your God.*' Private praise and worship of God, a deep sense of indebtedness to Him, a delight in speaking to Him and learning of Him, a readiness to do anything for Him, an overriding concern to be pleasing to Him – these are the means of preventing any desire forming for the old life, and for the attractions of a fallen world.

Then there are verses of warning from verse 12 to the end of this twenty-third chapter, showing the necessity of biblical separation from worldliness, a doctrine largely ignored by the 'isms' of today, such as large parts of the charismatic movement and the so-called church growth movement. If we are drawn back into the world, says Joshua, we will become backsliders and fall away from God's favour and blessing. We should read these verses with worldly entertainments and habits in our mind, and even with contemporary

Josh 23.12-24.15

Christian worship in view. Joshua warns about relaxing love for the Lord in favour of admiration for worldly things in these words:–

'Else if ye do in any wise go back, and cleave unto the remnant of these nations, even these that remain among you, and shall make marriages with them, and go in unto them, and they to you: know for a certainty that the Lord your God will no more drive out any of these nations from before you; but they shall be snares and traps unto you, and scourges in your sides, and thorns in your eyes, until ye perish from off this good land which the Lord your God hath given you' *(Joshua 23.12-13).*

Worldly compromises and indulgence will be 'scourges in your sides', bringing in due time much pain, and eliminating true joy in the Lord. Worldly ways will be 'thorns in your eyes', so that we will not be able to see spiritual things as we once did, because we will be under the discipline of God, even as believers. To 'perish quickly from off the good land' (verse 16) does not mean that believers will forfeit their salvation, but like the Israelites of old they will know times of barrenness, often being ruled by their enemies.

The Importance of Serving the Lord

'Joshua gathered all the tribes of Israel to Shechem, and called for the elders of Israel, and for their heads, and for their judges, and for their officers; and they presented themselves before God. And Joshua said unto all the people . . . ' *(Joshua 24.1-2).*

We assume that the great assembly of chapter 24 is a continuation of the one called by the aging leader in chapter 23. Joshua's address

Josh 24

to the people is a God-honouring rehearsal of their glorious history, calculated to deepen their trust and enlarge their sense of indebtedness and responsibility. Sixteen times in these verses the Lord says, 'I' did this and that, and we must apply this to our salvation, for Christ has done everything to purchase us, and the Holy Spirit has drawn us to light and repentance. We owe everything to God.

The hornets (of verse 12) which the Lord sent ahead of Joshua's troops, to drive out their enemy, were either literal hornets, or (as they are not mentioned in the narratives of the conflict) are a figure for inexplicable fear and panic put into the foe by God. Either way, it was the Lord Who won every engagement, and although the Israelites used their weapons, the words of the Lord show the reality, that their victories were 'not with thy sword, nor with thy bow'.

Grace is the crowning theme of verse 13, 'And I have given you a land for which ye did not labour, and cities which ye built not, and ye dwell in them . . .' The vital conclusion comes in verse 14 – 'Now therefore fear the Lord, and serve him in sincerity and in truth.' From this verse to verse 22 there are fourteen exhortations to 'serve'.

Sometimes the word 'serve' is translated from the Hebrew word for worship, but here, on all fourteen occasions, it is the Hebrew word 'work'. Repeatedly we read, 'Work for the Lord! Work for the Lord!' Three times the exhortation appears as 'Work *only* for Him!' Do not divide your energies. Do not put even your family before the Lord. Of course we must look after our families and our children and care for them, but we must never make idols of them, lavishing more love and attention on them than we do on the things of the Lord. It is the Lord Who must come first in all matters, not our possessions, not our success in life, or anything else.

Evangelicalism has so changed over recent decades that the opposite is assumed today, as Christians are taught to put family, career, appearances, worldly leisure and possessions before the service of God. The people of Joshua's time were tempted to put temporal things first, and so he challenges them with famous words: 'If it seem evil unto you to serve the Lord, choose you this day whom ye will serve' (verse 15). 'If you think anything is better or more important than the Lord,' he says, 'then you go and serve that. If you think that God is unreasonable to you, go and serve something else.' Of course, they recoiled from this terrible proposal, and then Joshua challenged them even more, uttering his own famous pledge: 'As for me and my house, we will serve the Lord.' Joshua, their great and

(Josh 24.15-22) godly leader, firm and stable as a mighty rock, shows his own sanctified heart in these words, 'Choose you this day . . .' For him, life was a succession of choices, as day by day and hour by hour he chose the standards and service of the Lord. If there was a predominant element in his faithfulness, it is surely to be found in this word 'choose', and we should learn from this. Does something essentially selfish and self-serving appeal to us? A choice is to be made. Whatever inner urge may carry us into unworthy and sinful conduct, a choice is to be made, and Joshua brings the work of mortification and godliness down to this.

The people responded to Joshua, saying, 'God forbid that we should forsake the Lord, to serve other gods.' Did they mean it, or was their response more of an emotional reaction? Tragically events were to prove that while they partly meant it, their pledge was largely sentimental.

It is vital that there should be sentiment in our responses to the Lord, but we must make sure they are not only sentiment. It is possible to be moved when we sing a hymn, but to have no accompanying deep intention of obeying the Lord. Often we may be moved as we pray, saying, 'Lord take my life,' but we do not really give it to Him. We continue to do things of which He would not approve, or which are all for our earthly benefit, and we fail to do much for Him. The grand statement of commitment made by the Israelites turned out to be largely sentimental, because with the lapse of one generation after the death of Joshua, they were to fall away on a tragic scale.

Shallow Faith Defined

There is an inherent problem in the response to Joshua made by the Israelites, and one so serious that we quote their words in full: 'For the Lord our God, he it is that brought us up and our fathers out of the land of Egypt, from the house of bondage, and which did those great signs in our sight, and preserved us in all the way wherein we went, and among all the people through whom we passed: and the Lord drave out from before us all the people, even the Amorites which dwelt in the land: therefore will we also serve the Lord; for he is our God' *(Joshua 24.17-18)*.

Their stated reason for serving the Lord was entirely correct as far as it went, echoing in measure what Joshua had said to them, but unfortunately it went no further than *benefits* they had received. We will serve the Lord, they said, because of what He has done for us, and all that He has given us, and (by implication) all that He will do for us. They think of all their material blessings on earth, but they do not see behind these to admire *Him*, and to adore His matchless attributes, His kindness and His love.

What would happen when the first drought came along, and other difficulties arose? They would apostatise, because the only reason they served the Lord was that they gained so much from Him. In their reply we see the shallowness of their commitment, and we go on to challenge ourselves.

It is good to praise the Lord for our salvation, His mercy upon us and His great deliverances. Of course, we must praise Him for these things, but there is much more. We must wonder at and admire His holiness, His love, His power, His knowledge and His mercy. We must want Him not just for the glorious things He does for us on earth, but because this is right, and He is God, and He is glorious, and He is the One Who made us. We must love Him because He has given us eternity to gaze upon Him. The answer of the Israelites was shallow and inadequate, having only one ingredient, their benefits, and this would never sustain their loyalty in the future.

Joshua accordingly warns them – 'Ye cannot serve the Lord: for he is an holy God; he is a jealous God' (verse 19). He will not be indifferent to your drifting away from Him. If you forsake Him to serve strange gods, then He will have to deal with you very severely. But the people said, 'No, no, no. We will serve the Lord!'

Nevertheless Joshua makes them vow very solemnly that they

(Josh 24.22-33) mean what they say, and he makes them enter into a covenant, and then puts up a monument (as God commanded) to mark what they have said. All these acts are an example for us today. When people genuinely come to the Lord, we baptise them, as Christ commanded. This does not do anything for them, but it is a significant, God-given sign that the old life is dead and new life has come. In future the believer will look back and say, 'I pledged myself to the Lord that day because of what He had done in my life, and because He brought me to appreciate Him and love Him.' Then the believer comes into church membership, and certain pledges and undertakings are connected with that, and the scriptural right-hand of fellowship is extended. All these acts help believers to be serious in their commitment, but they cannot help if a person's commitment to the Lord was shallow in the first place, and only based on the benefits, wonderful as they are.

The words of verse 31 bring the book to an end on a rather sad note: 'Israel served the Lord all the days of Joshua, and all the days of the elders that overlived Joshua.' We cannot help but notice that the elders who outlived Joshua are mentioned, not the elders who succeeded them. It would seem that a good spiritual tone persisted for only a few years (perhaps up to 30 years) before decline began, leading to the horrors recorded in the last chapters of *Judges*. (Those final chapters describe a period between Joshua and the Judges.)

Loyalty needs far more than gratitude and love for what the Lord has done for us. That is good, but something deeper is needed. Let us love Him for *Who He is*, and *what He is like*, and for *His greatness* and *majesty*, and *kindness*, and *mercy*, and *knowledge*, and *power*. We see Him most clearly in the Lord Jesus Christ, the eternal Son, Who is glorious.

We love Him also because He has shed love abroad in our hearts; a love as mysterious as that in human courtship and marriage, and yet infinitely better founded in His person and work. It is a love full of appreciation, esteem, admiration, desire, and a readiness to obey, but more, it is an indescribable love. Yet our personal sense of this love must grow and be expressed daily, and must be kept undiluted by love of the world or self-love, for it is the only way to lasting loyalty. Perhaps the best view of Joshua the man is reserved to this twenty-fourth chapter, where we see his strong awareness of privilege and accountability to God, his unwavering loyalty, his determination to stand apart from the Canaanite world, his tireless commitment to the Lord's work, and his sincere love for the Lord. This kind of life is ultimately the message of *Joshua*.

The Mutual Love of Christ and His People

An explanation of the *Song of Solomon* for personal devotions and Bible study groups

115 pages, paperback, ISBN 1 870855 40 X

The courtship of the *Song of Solomon* provides fascinating scenes and events designed to show the love of Christ for His redeemed people, and theirs for Him. Here, also, are lessons for Christians when they become cold or backslidden, showing the way to recover Christ's presence in their lives.

Prophecies of Christ abound in the *Song*, together with views of the bride's destiny, as she prepares to cross the mountains into eternal glory, where the greatest wedding of all will take place.

This book begins with a brief overview of the reasons why the *Song* should be seen as allegorical – the viewpoint held throughout church history by the overwhelming majority of preachers and commentators. Then, in verse-by-verse mode, but designed for continuous devotional reading, the symbols are explained and applied.

Testimonies to the blessing obtained through this treatment of the *Song* have come from all over the world, from ministers and 'lay' people alike.

Not Like Any Other Book

161 pages, paperback, ISBN 1 870855 43 4

Faulty Bible interpretation lies at the root of every major mistake and 'ism' assailing churches today, and countless Christians are asking for the old, traditional and proven way of handling the Bible to be spelled out plainly.

A new approach to interpretation has also gripped many evangelical seminaries and Bible colleges, an approach based on the ideas of unbelieving critics, stripping the Bible of God's message, and leaving pastors impoverished in their preaching.

This book reveals what is happening, providing many brief examples of right and wrong interpretation. The author shows that the Bible includes its own rules of interpretation, and every believer should know what these are.

God's Rules for Holiness
Unlocking the Ten Commandments
139 pages, paperback, ISBN 1 870855 37 X

Taken at face value the Ten Commandments are binding on all people, and will guard the way to Heaven, so that evil will never spoil its glory and purity. But the Commandments are far greater than their surface meaning, as this book shows.

They challenge us as Christians on a still wider range of sinful deeds and attitudes. They provide positive virtues as goals. And they give immense help for staying close to the Lord in our walk and worship.

The Commandments are vital for godly living and for greater blessing, but we need to enter into the panoramic view they provide for the standards and goals for redeemed people.

The Lord's Pattern for Prayer
118 pages, paperback, ISBN 1 870855 36 1

Subtitled – 'Studying the lessons and spiritual encouragements in the most famous of all prayers.' This volume is almost a manual on prayer, providing a real spur to the devotional life. The Lord's own plan and agenda for prayer – carefully amplified – takes us into the presence of the Father, to prove the privileges and power of God's promises to those who pray.

Chapters cover each petition in the Lord's Prayer. Here, too, are sections on remedies for problems in prayer, how to intercede for others, the reasons why God keeps us waiting for answers, and the nature of the prayer of faith.

Heritage of Evidence

127 pages, illustrated, paperback, ISBN 1 870855 39 6

In today's atheistic climate most people have no idea how much powerful evidence exists for the literal accuracy and authenticity of the biblical record. The British Museum holds a huge number of major discoveries that provide direct corroboration and background confirmation for an immense sweep of Bible history. This survey of Bible-authenticating exhibits has been designed as a guide for visitors, and also to give pleasure and interest to readers unable to tour the galleries. It will also be most suitable for people who need to see the accuracy and inspiration of the Bible.

The 'tour' followed here started life over forty years ago and has been used by many thousands of people including youth and student groups.

Almost every item viewed on the tour receives a full colour photograph. Room plans are provided for every gallery visited showing the precise location of artefacts, and time-charts relate the items to contemporary kings and prophets. The book is enriched by pictures and descriptions of famous 'proofs' in other museums.

Men of Purpose

157 pages, illustrated, paperback, ISBN 1 870855 41 8

This book brings into one illustrated volume eleven great lives, all with an experience of personal conversion to God. Composer Mendelssohn, food industrialist Henry Heinz, novelist Daniel Defoe, and some of the most celebrated scientists of all time, are among the examples of leading people whose lives were changed by a sight of real Christianity. Also very suitable as a gift to unconverted friends, and to enrich sermons and Bible class messages.

Physicians of Souls
The Gospel Ministry
285 pages, paperback, ISBN 1 870855 34 5

'Compelling, convicting, persuasive preaching, revealing God's mercy and redemption to dying souls, is seldom heard today. The noblest art ever granted to our fallen human race has almost disappeared.'

Even where the free offer of the Gospel is treasured in principle, regular evangelistic preaching has become a rarity, contends the author. These pages tackle the inhibitions, theological and practical, and provide powerful encouragement for physicians of souls to preach the Gospel. A vital anatomy or order of conversion is supplied with advice for counselling seekers.

The author shows how passages for evangelistic persuasion may be selected and prepared. He also challenges modern church growth techniques, showing the superiority of direct proclamation. These and other key topics make up a complete guide to soul-winning.

Worship in the Melting Pot
148 pages, paperback, ISBN 1 870855 33 7

'Worship is truly in the melting pot,' says the author. 'A new style of praise has swept into evangelical life shaking to the foundations traditional concepts and attitudes.' How should we react? Is it all just a matter of taste and age? Will churches be helped, or changed beyond recognition?

This book presents four essential principles which Jesus Christ laid down for worship, and by which every new idea must be judged.

Here also is a fascinating view of how they worshipped in Bible times, including their rules for the use of instruments, and the question is answered – What does the Bible teach about the content and order of a service of worship today?

Do We Have a Policy?
For church health and growth
93 pages, paperback, ISBN 1 870855 30 2

Only One Baptism of the Holy Spirit
109 pages, paperback, ISBN 1 870855 17 5

The Healing Epidemic
227 pages, paperback, ISBN 1 870855 00 0

The Charismatic Phenomenon *[co-authored with John C. Whitcomb]*
113 pages, paperback, ISBN 1 870855 01 9

Steps for Guidance
184 pages, paperback, ISBN 1 870855 19 1

Biblical Strategies for Witness
126 pages, paperback, ISBN 1 870855 18 3

Should Christians Drink?
112 pages, paperback, ISBN 1 870855 12 4

www.wakemantrust.org